Governing Ethnic Conflict

This book offers an intellectual history of an emerging technology of peace and explains how the liberal state has come to endorse illiberal subjects and practices.

The idea that conflicts are problems that have causes and therefore solutions rather than winners and losers has gained momentum since the end of the Cold War, and it has become more common for third-party mediators acting in the name of liberal internationalism to promote the resolution of intra-state conflicts. These third-party peace makers appear to share lessons and expertise so that it is possible to speak of an emergent common technology of peace based around a controversial form of power-sharing known as consociation.

In this common technology of peace, the cause of conflict is understood to be competing ethno-national identities and the solution is to recognise these identities, and make them useful to government through power-sharing. Drawing on an analysis of the peace process in Ireland and the Dayton Accords in Bosnia-Herzegovina, the book argues that the problem with consociational arrangements is not simply that they institutionalise ethnic division and privilege particular identities or groups, but, more importantly, that they close down the space for other ways of being. By specifying identity categories, consociational regimes create a residual category, designated 'other'. These 'others' not only offer a challenge to prevailing ideas about identity but also stand in reproach to conventional wisdom regarding the management of conflict.

This book will be of much interest to students of conflict resolution, ethnic conflict, identity, and war and conflict studies in general.

Andrew Finlay is Lecturer in Sociology at Trinity College, Dublin.

Routledge studies in peace and conflict resolution

Series editors: Tom Woodhouse and Oliver Ramsbotham
University of Bradford

Governing Ethnic Conflict
Consociation, identity and the price of peace

Andrew Finlay

 Routledge
Taylor & Francis Group

LONDON AND NEW YORK

First published 2011
by Routledge
2 Park Square, Milton Park, Abingdon, Oxon, OX14 4RN

Simultaneously published in the USA and Canada
by Routledge
711 Third Avenue, New York, NY 10017

Routledge is an imprint of the Taylor & Francis Group, an informa business

First issued in paperback 2011

© 2011 Andrew Finlay

Typeset in Times New Roman by Swales & Willis Ltd, Exeter, Devon

British Library Cataloguing in Publication Data
A catalogue record for this book is available from the British Library

Library of Congress Cataloging-in-Publication Data
Finlay, Andrew.
   Governing ethnic conflict: consociation, identity, and the price of peace / Andrew Finlay
   p. cm.
   1. Ethnic conflict. 2. Ethnicity—Political aspects. 3. State, The.
   4. Cultural pluralism. I. Title.
   HM1121.F56 2010
   305.8001—dc22
   2010002332

ISBN13: 978–0–415–49803–6 (hbk)
ISBN13: 978–0–203–84731–2 (ebk)
ISBN13: 978–0–415–51011–0 (pbk)

To Margaret and the memory of Vera and Roy

Contents

Abbreviations

AAI	Anglo-Irish Agreement, 1985
CTG	Cultural Traditions Group
ECHR	European Convention for Human Rights
ETA	Euskadi Ta Askatasuna
GFA	Good Friday Agreement, 1998
IRA	Irish Republican Army
NIHRC	Northern Ireland Human Rights Commission
NILP	Northern Ireland Labour Party
OFMDFM	Office of the First Minister and Deputy First Minister
PR	Proportional Representation
PUP	Progressive Unionist Party
SACHR	The Standing Advisory Commission on Human Rights
SDLP	Social Democratic and Labour Party
UDA	Ulster Defence Association
UNESCO	United Nations Educational, Scientific and Cultural Organisation
UVF	Ulster Volunteer Force

Preface and acknowledgements

'More punk less folk!' This was the response of a Bosnian community relations worker to a sceptical remark I had made about treating culture as both the cause of conflict and its solution. He described the 'typical . . . "successful" interethnic (intercultural) project' favoured by 'international donors' as one that ended 'with a blend of folklore[s] . . . we sing each other songs, tell . . . jokes'. For him, this kind of project was anything but successful: 'from my perspective, this is just a reproduction/reinforcement of differences'. The kind of cultural project he would like to develop if only he could get the funds would be based in '"alternative" (underground, countercultural, OFF, call it as you like) cultural paradigms, which offer . . . additional points of identification, potential (not necessary) transcendence of ethnic identity'. He thought that working with youth was particularly important because they had been raised in an 'ideological' environment where ethnicity was paramount. Hence: 'more punk less folk!' (personal communication, 4 December 2009 and 12 December 2009).

The community relations worker's remarks should not be dismissed as fanciful. Think of the role played by the 'alternative cultural' scene in Belgrade in the huge protests against the Milosevic regime in 1996 and 1997. Stef Jansen describes alternative music as a 'vector of dissent' (see Jansen 2001: 49) during those protests, and there is evidence that it continues to play this role, albeit at a much lower pitch (Murphy 2008). But, the community relations worker quoted above was under no illusions. He was modest about what he thought his preferred inter-cultural, community relations programme might achieve:

> if BiH (Bosnia-Herzegovina) is doomed to a post-war reconciliation intervention, and it seems it is, let's be innovative, introduce some new . . . social, cultural . . . practices into those communities in small scales of

course. This kind of approach would not . . . transform the whole society
into heaven of peace, it simply introduce[s] new 'signifiers'.

(personal communication, 12 December 2009)

In any case, he was reconciled that this kind of programme was unlikely to
attract funding from international donors; more's the pity.

There are some who have illusions about the punk scene in Northern
Ireland in the late 1970s and 1980s as a kind of community relations programme *avant la lettre*. Martin McLoone (2004) has characterised this as
'punk nostalgia': an indulgence on the part of a generation of old punks
who now occupy influential positions in the media. The political context
of the nostalgia he diagnoses is precise: several years after the signing of a
peace agreement, and it appeared that sectarian or ethnic divisions, especially amongst the working class, were worse than ever. There is, he suggests, a nostalgic longing for the opportunity that punk music once offered
of, 'an imagining beyond a sectarian politics, a rebellion against the complacent certainties of a sectarian political culture that had delivered nothing
but social disharmony and communal breakdown' (McLoone 2004: 32).
Henry McDonald (2004) has written of a 'spirit of rebellion and personal
freedom unleashed in that brief but important flowering of Belfast "counter
culture"'.

Against this, there are those who would argue that a haircut is the easi-
est form of rebellion. Des Bell has argued that it was the youth, often with
Mohican haircuts and leather jackets and punk music, who re-invigorated
'traditional' loyalist politics in the 1980s and 1990s (Bell 1990 and 1996).
Bill Rolston has pointed out that, with one or two exceptions, the message
of punk bands was 'remarkably tame' politically (2001: 65), and that this
was precisely because 'groups played to young people from both sides of
the political divide': they could not afford to alienate half their audience. He
concludes that the notion of punk music as the beginning 'of a new cross-
community youth culture that would lead to an end of the conflict' was fanciful (2001: 59).

My experience of punk in Belfast in the 1970s and 1980s would tend to
support the analysis of Bell and Rolston. I recall the derision with which a
very good friend (still) responded to my suggestion that we go to see a fairly
well-known English punk band (my memory fails me here – I can't remember which one), who were playing a 'rock the [H] block' gig in West Belfast
as part of a broader campaign for political status for republican prisoners. I
also recall the hostility with which friends at the Harp Bar, then epicentre of
the punk scene, met the suggestion (the source of which I cannot remember),

that we should create a 'rock against sectarianism' on the lines of rock against racism in Britain.

And yet, this is not to dismiss the significance of punk. My guess is that escapism was probably the main thing for most, and this escapist spirit was not unique to punk. Nor was punk unique in its ability to bring together 'large numbers of young people from different backgrounds, with kids from Catholic and Protestant areas mixing together freely without fear or intimidation' (O'Neill and Trelford 2003, quoted in Campbell 2007). Punk was not an aberration, but one of a sequence of underground scenes based around different genres of music that ebbed and flowed after punk (and before it too I am sure): hi energy, electro, dance music – Belfast had its own 'summer of love' in the early 1990s (see also Rolston 2001: 66 note 25).

In the context of a post-conflict society in which the underlying logic appears to be that 'good fences make good neighbours', 'punk nostalgia' is seductive and should be resisted. But with distance, it is also too easy to dismiss punk's significance. In any case, what should not be underestimated is the value in an ethnically divided society of bringing together people on the basis of a shared interest or activity where their ethnic identity is not the highest virtue. In the words of the Bosnian community relations worker mentioned earlier, the alternative inter-cultural projects he would develop if he were given the chance would have the modest aims of 'creating additional points of identification, potential (not necessary) transcendence of ethnic identity' (personal communication, 4 December 2009; see also Pickering 2006).

To which I would add the modest aim of encouraging friendships. Leela Gandhi in her book, *Affective Communities: Anticolonial Thought, Fin-de-Siècle Radicalism, and the Politics of Friendship*, argues for the importance of 'those invisible affective gestures that refuse alignment along the secure axis of filiation to seek expression outside, if not against possessive communities of belonging' (Gandhi 2006: 10). I say 'modest', because friendship is not innocent of power, and as Begona Aretxaga has argued: 'any readiness to model political relationships on the principle of friendship requires awareness that there can be no good friendship when a fluid negotiation of power differentials in the relationship is lacking' (2005: 282).

I am still friends with many of the people I met through Belfast's 'counterculture': they remain my 'affective community'. So my first acknowledgement is to them, and to the places where we met: the Harp Bar, the Pound, Dubarry's, Lavery's, Jules, the Delta and the Plaza ballrooms (run by Ernie and Jim – two of the unsung heroes), the Carpenters, Just Books, the Anarchy Centre, the Crescent Centre, the Midlands, the Rathcoole Self Help Group, Sugar Sweet, Choice.

Amongst other things, this book offers a genealogy of a particular approach to peace agreement and conflict resolution, exemplified by the Good Friday Agreement and the Dayton Accords. As befits a book concerned with intellectual history, the research draws largely on documentary sources produced by international organisations, government departments, non-governmental organisations, and academics and consultants of various kinds. While much material is now available online via the Internet, libraries remain crucial, and not just for the obscure stuff. I would like to thank staff at Northern Ireland Political Section of the Linen Hall Library, Belfast and in the library at Trinity College, Dublin – especially the Inter library Loans Section – for their help and advice.

It was the literature on the Dayton Accords, especially the critical literature, that inspired me to work on this book, and it has benefited from several trips to Bosnia-Herzegovina and conversations with some of the authors of this literature: academics, journalists and community/civil society activists. I am grateful to Nicholas Whyte of Independent Diplomat, Allan Little of the British Broadcasting Corporation and Elana Haviv of the Children's Movement for Creative Education for introducing me to people in Bosnia-Herzegovina. Of the various people that I met, I would especially like to thank Asim Mujkic, Ugo Vlaisavljevic and Dino Abazović of the University of Sarajevo; Svjetlana Nedimović, Edin Hodžić and Tarik Jusić of *Puls demokratije*; Adnan Ramic; Ivona Letic; Ismet Lisica, drafters of the *Youth Constitution of Bosnia and Herzegovina*; and Nebojsa Savija-Valha of the Nansen Dialogue Centre, Sarajevo. My visits to Bosnia-Herzegovina were made possible by funding from the Higher Education Authority, Programme for Research and in Third Level Institutions (PRTLI) though the Global Networks Project, Institute for International Integration Studies at Trinity College, Dublin.

In addition to the work conducted as part of the Global Networks Project, the book also draws on various other bits and pieces of research conducted in Northern Ireland over the years. With this in mind I would like to acknowledge the support at various times of the Department of Education for Northern Ireland, the Amalgamated Transport and General Workers Union and the Arts and Benefaction Fund at Trinity College, Dublin. I would also like to thank Dick Hunter for making available to me the transcript of his interviews with Jack Macgougan.

I owe a particular debt to Mick O'Broin who I was lucky enough to have as a Research Assistant for a short time, paid for by the Higher Education Authority, Programme for Research and in Third Level Institutions through the Global Networks Project. Mick also read and commented on an early draft of this book, and I am grateful to him for his comments on the draft and for the ongoing conversation. Likewise Robin Whitaker who also read and commented on an early draft of the book.

It was Marie Smyth who suggested I try submitting my book proposal to Andrew Humphrys at Routledge, so thanks to her for that. Thanks also to Máiréad Nic Craith and Helena Wulff who read and offered very useful comments on a draft of the book proposal. Comments made by the anonymous referees and the series editors, Tom Woodhouse and Oliver Ramsbotham were also very useful. Thanks are also due to Andrew Humphrys and Rebecca Brennan for their help in the preparation of the manuscript. Any errors are my own.

Finally, thanks to Orla O'Brien for her kindness and support throughout this writing project.

1   Introduction

The idea that conflicts are problems that have causes and therefore solutions (rather than winners and losers) is a quintessentially modern idea, but its application to intra-state conflicts was belated. The delay is usually attributed to the Cold War, when the international community was less concerned with ending civil wars than with the possibility of world war (see Ramsbotham *et al.* 2005 and Pugh 2002). Since the end of the Cold War it has become more and more common for third-party mediators to intervene in intra-state conflicts in the name of liberal internationalism (see McGrew 2002). These third-party peace makers – United Nations agencies, small neutral states and non-governmental organisations – have done much to promote the idea that conflicts can be resolved or at least managed; peace kept, made and built. They also appear to share lessons and expertise (Darby and MacGinty 2003). Bell (2008: 105) suggests that a common set of techniques for peace-making is emerging such that 'peace agreements across conflicts evidence strikingly similar arrangements and devices (or "frameworks") for accommodating the competing demands of the conflict's protagonists'.

The intellectual history or genealogy of this emerging common approach to peace-making is what concerns me here. My case studies are the Good Friday Agreement (GFA, Northern Ireland 1998[1]) and to a lesser extent the Dayton Accords (Bosnia-Herzegovina 1995). I'll explain my approach to intellectual history and the significance of these case studies in a moment, but let me begin by sketching the common technology of peace-making.

If there is a common technology of peace, its self-styled 'engineers' are 'consociationalists' (see Lijphart 1995 and McGarry and O'Leary 1995). Consociationalism is a theory developed mainly within political science. Some have claimed it to be the 'dominant' or 'default' response of the international community when it comes to conflict resolution (see Taylor 2009; Anderson 2006). Consociation is conventionally described as the sharing of power between the leaders of the contending groups or segments (Lijphart 1977), each of which usually granted power of veto. But it might be just as accurate to describe consociation as the disaggregation of power (Bell 2008) for it also involves the proportional distribution of posts not just in the executive, but in the legislature and bureaucracy such that these cannot be dominated by any one group. And consociational agreements grant autonomy to each of the contending groups: self-rule in 'matters of profound cultural consequence, with the institutional recognition that principle entails' (O'Leary 2006: xviii).

The influence of consociational theory can be seen not just in the GFA and the Dayton Accords but in many of the key peace agreements of the recent period; for example, the Ta'if Accords (Lebanon 1989), the South African interim constitution (1993–96), the Ohrid Agreement (Macedonia 2000) and the Iraqi constitution (2005). But we should note that each of these agreements have provisions above and beyond those inscribed in consociational theory. The common technology of peace usually includes human rights provisions, community relations policies, arrangements for policing, the decommissioning of weapons and dealing with the past; though the latter has proved especially problematic. More than that, some of these agreements begin to redefine the state, sovereignty, belonging and citizenship in quite novel ways.

As Bell argues, these peace agreements are 'not merely a common set of conflict resolution techniques, but . . . a distinctive form of constitutionalism' (2008: 287). To which we might add: there is more to the emergent technology of peace than consociation. If I use this awkward term and its derivatives it is for convenience and for want of a better one. The shorthand is permissible if we remember that actually existing consociational agreements involve more than power sharing, proportionality and cultural autonomy.

My training is in anthropology not political science or law, so what prompted me to study the intellectual history of this form of peace-making? Something like a consociationalism had been tried in Northern Ireland in 1974 (the 'Sunningdale Agreement'), which made the place a test case for consociational theory. I don't remember that well, but later on in the 1980s when I was working in trade union and cross-community projects I remember being puzzled when the government began to invest large resources in projects that seemed to endorse communalism: work with what were to become known as 'single-identity' groups. The liberal state appeared to endorse forms of conflict resolution and community relations work that ran counter to liberal principles. I wasn't the only one to be puzzled, and the apparent contradictions gave rise to a critique and a response that has become increasingly tired and routinised. So in addition to offering an intellectual history of an influential approach to peace-making, I hope this book will also illuminate a puzzle and contribute towards a more productive critique. And it turns out that anthropological conceptions of culture and what is now called identity are central to both of these tasks.

In the 1990s a new generation of consociational revisionists, led by John McGarry and Brendan O'Leary, pitched themselves against the liberal analysis of ethnic conflict as an expression of backwardness or regression and against the liberal prescription for dealing with ethnic conflict; namely integration. 'The goal of liberals is straightforward', say McGarry and O'Leary (2004: 169; first published 1995): 'the erosion of ethnic solidarities, at least in the public realm and the promotion of a more rational state and society based on equal individual rights'. Against this, consociational prescriptions assert that ethnic groups exist and have rights.

The literature on the pros and cons of consociation is large and not all of the criticism comes from 'liberals'. As Christopher McCrudden acknowledges many of the critics are from 'left . . . and feminist traditions', but he still refers to the critique as 'liberal' (2007: 316–17) and it is true that, whatever the ideological position of the critic, the fundamental criticism is similar. The fundamental problem with consociational peace agreements is that they entrench or institutionalise ethnic divisions and thereby sustain antagonism or at least inhibit reconciliation (Langhammer 2000; McCann 2001; Finlay 2001a and 2004; Horowitz 2001; Taylor 2001; Finlay 2004; McVeigh and Rolston 2007; Wilson 2009b; Farry 2009). Some of the critics go further and argue that this defect in consociational agreements is the expression of a defect in consociational theory, which 'assumes that identities are primordial and exclusive rather than malleable and relational'(Wilson and Wilford 2003: 6).

The consociational riposte is equally straightforward. McGarry and O'Leary (2004: 32) argue that 'there is a major difference between thinking that identities are durable and maintaining that they are immutably primordial'; that is, some kind of cultural essence handed down intact from the ancestors generation after generation. 'Liberals' may not like it, but the fact is that ethnicity is durable and a force to be reckoned with. The 'institutional accommodation of rival groups' can bring peace and an 'extensive period of cooperation between them is more likely to transform identities in the long run than any . . . [liberal] integrationist options' (McGarry 2001: 124). John McGarry calls this 'the consociational paradox'.

The rhetorical opposition between consociationalism and liberalism now seems odd given that for practical purposes consociationalism has become the liberal state's default approach to conflict resolution. From an anthropological perspective, the debate seems even stranger. Consociational theorists wish to hold on to the notion that the conflicts with which they are concerned are conflicts of ethnic or ethno-national identity, but so keen have they become to avoid the taint of primordialism that they disavow the culture concept altogether and retreat further into 'new institutionalism'; that is, an emphasis on the socio-structural rather than the cultural roots of conflict. I found this attempted disavowal of culture interesting because it flew in the face of what I already knew about the pioneer of consociational theory, Arend Lijphart, and of my experience of actually existing consociational agreements.

Chapter 2, goes back to Lijphart's work and shows the importance of both anthropological theory and the case of Northern Ireland to the early development of consociational theory and practice. For Lijphart, Northern Ireland is 'the most unambiguous instance of a plural society . . . in the Western world' (1977: 134), and anthropologists were then the foremost theorists of plural society. We find that Lijphart was frank about the debt he owed to anthropological approaches to pluralism, including cultural pluralism, and indeed to primordialism. We trace his subsequent efforts, and those of the younger generation of consociational 'revisionists', to distance themselves from a primordial or essentialist view of ethno-national identity by developing a consociational practice that would allow people to determine their own identities. In line with this they elaborate a distinction between 'corporate' consociations typified by the Dayton Accords and 'liberal' consociations typified by the GFA. The chapter ends by looking at the GFA, and showing how far short it falls of liberal ideals: people in Northern Ireland have no right to individual self-determination, self-identification, or even of exit from their designated ethno-national group. Ethnicity seems normative.

And yet these peace agreements continue to enjoy the support of the liberal state. How so? This question is approached in Chapter 3. To answer it, we take a wider perspective than consociational theory and practice, and look at the history of the pluralism upon which it ultimately draws. Crucial here is what Susan Wright (1998) has referred to as the 'old' anthropological idea of culture. The 'old' idea of culture is associated with a relativistic view of a world made up of discrete peoples, each with their own distinct way of life. In this worldview, cultures are spatially located and based on inherited meanings that are shared equally by all the members of the culture. This concept of culture justifies a conflation of individual and collective communal identity such that the former is understood as dependent on the latter. The respect that liberalism traditionally accords to the individual is thereby extended to the group of which s/he is a member. Irrespective of the revisionist disavowal, it is precisely this concept of culture that enables the liberal state to embrace the theory and practice of group autonomy that consociationalism shares with liberal multiculturalism.

Implicit in these two chapters is an approach to intellectual history derived from Foucault, known as genealogy. In line with this approach, my reason for tracing the implicit reliance of consociationalism on pluralist theory and notions of cultural identity isn't because I favour culturalist explanation of ethno-national conflict, still less because I wish to replace an 'old' outmoded concept of culture with a better one. In line with Foucault's genealogical approach to intellectual history, I do not regard the human sciences as some separate scholarly realm in which knowledge progresses though a cumulative process of research and theorisation. Rather I am interested in the relationship between knowledge and power within the human sciences, and the influence of these sciences on the practice of peace-making. Genealogy is a form of critique, but it is not unremittingly negative. Yes, power is understood to work through the regulation of behaviour, but it is not only repressive: power is also understood as productive, working by influencing conduct and through subject formation and identification.

In this approach 'identity' is understood as a matter of government not culture, though cultural identity is the current regime of the person through which government works (Rose 1996). By foregrounding power/knowledge and understanding it as a productive potential, genealogy enables us to create some movement in a debate about consociational peace agreements that has become tired.

It is at this juncture that the Dayton Accords begin to figure more in the discussion. As case studies in consociationalism, the Dayton Accords and the GFA are a good pair: the former as an example of what consociational theorists call a corporate consociation and the latter as an example of liberal consociation. When possible I draw comparisons between these peace agreements, their implementation and their critique, but I hesitate to call this a comparative study. My hesitation is twofold, stemming from an anthropological appreciation of the importance of context and language. First, while the two peace agreements share in an emergent common technology of peace, the conflicts which they sought to end have very different histories and drawing parallels here is a dubious enterprise (see Brendan Simms n.d.). Second, I do not know Bosnian with the obvious limitations in terms of both written sources and who I could and could not speak with when I visited the former Yugoslavia.[2] More than anything else, the literature coming out of Bosnia-Herzegovina in English has been a source of inspiration: the critique of the Dayton Accords seems richer and more assertive than the critique of the GFA, and it provided the starting point for the analysis developed from Chapter 4 on.

It was while reading the literature on the Dayton Accords that I hit upon the notion of 'normative ethnicity', though Paul Gilroy's 'ethnic absolutism' (1990) was also significant. Chapter 4 starts with a quote from Asim Mujkic, a Bosnian political philosopher who describes ethnopolitics as a form of biopolitics. The term 'biopolitics' is taken from Foucault's *History of Sexuality* (1980). Biopolitics, together with the term 'biopower', alludes to forms of politics that are concerned with the population, its well-being and reproduction or survival. In Chapter 4 we discuss the relevance of these terms to Northern Ireland starting with the demographic arguments that fed into the peace process. This leads to a discussion of censuses, employment legislation and the elaboration of official practices and techniques whereby individuals can be allocated to ethnic groups without their consent. These techniques are subsequently elevated to constitutional status in the rules inscribed in the GFA that require members elected to the new legislature to designate an identity as unionist, nationalist or 'other'. Throughout the chapter, the focus is on the expert knowledge and the claims to truth that underpin 'normative ethnicity'.

Foucault's discussion of biopower/biopolitics in the *History of Sexuality* is part of a larger genealogy of power in which he traces the emergence of a modern liberal governmentality that relies less on repression and coercion than on practices and programs that seek to influence conduct by 'cultivating particular types of individual and collective identity as well as forms of agency and subjectivity'(Inda 2005: 10). This is the productive potential of power/knowledge that I mentioned a moment ago. Chapter 5 explores the idea that consociationalism can be understood as a form of liberal governmentality.

In developing this argument we must confront again the old 'liberal' critique of consociation. In Chapters 2 and 4 we traced the development of policies that require the allocation of people to communal groups without their consent and force elected politicians to designate an identity. These developments would seem to confirm the 'old' critique of consociational agreements; that is that they institutionalise the ethnic or sectarian divisions that they are supposed to resolve. For the critics, the key indicator of the failure of consociation is that communal segregation increases following the signing of the peace agreement. The critics point to evidence such as the increase in the number of 'peace walls' dividing Catholics and protestants in Belfast. The evidence of failure is keenly disputed by the newer generation of revisionist consociationalists (see Taylor 2009).

The picture that emerges in Chapter 5 seems at first sight to be even more gloomy. Here we trace the development of an approach to community relations – known as 'single-identity' work – that seems to run counter to the stated purpose of the policy; namely the improvement of community relations through inter-ethnic dialogue.

Tracing the development of this approach to community relations, we can see that exponents of the 'old' critique of consociation are guilty of the same error that Foucault famously diagnosed in those who complained about the failure of the prison system to deter crime or rehabilitate offenders. In *Discipline and Punish*,[3] Foucault argues that the persistence of the prison system in the face of such a damning and effective critique suggests that while prisons might not achieve their stated purposes, they must serve some implicit function:

> perhaps one should reverse the problem and ask oneself what is served by the failure of the prison; what is the use of these different phenomena that are continually being criticized . . . Perhaps one should look for what is hidden beneath the apparent cynicism of the penal institution, which, after purging the convicts by means of their sentence, continues to follow them by a whole series of 'brandings' . . . and which thus pursues as a 'delinquent' someone who has acquitted himself of his punishment as an offender? Can we not see here a consequence rather than a contradiction? If so, we would be forced to suppose that the prison and no doubt punishment in general, is not intended to eliminate offences, but rather to distinguish them, to distribute them, to use them; that it is not so much that they render docile those who are liable to transgress the law, but that they tend to assimilate the transgression of the laws in a general tactics of subjection . . . Penalty would then appear to be a way of handling illegalities, of laying down the limits of tolerance, of giving free rein to some, of putting pressure on others, of excluding a particular section, of making another useful, of neutralizing certain individuals and of profiting from others. In short, penalty does not simply 'check' illegalities; it 'differentiates' them, it provides them with a general economy . . . the 'failure' of the prison system may be understood on this basis.
> (Foucault 1991: 272)

If the 'old' criticism of consociation is that it fails to resolve ethnic conflict so much as freeze it, we can now ask the Foucauldian question: what purpose does this supposed 'failure' achieve. In Chapter 3 I argue that what allows the liberal state to embrace the theory and practice of group autonomy whether in the form of multiculturalism or consociationalism is a culturalist confla-tion of individual and collective communal identity such that the former is understood as dependent on the latter. The respect that liberalism tradition-ally accords to the individual is thereby extended to the group of which s/he is a member. But if this is true – if our sense of self really does need to be sustained by a stable communal culture – ethnic identity is not merely a force to be reckoned with, it is a positive good!

In short, the argument of Chapter 5 is that consociation, as a form of liberal governmentality, is informed by and seeks to create ethno-national subjects through practices such as single-identity work and 'own culture validation'. Having traced the development of these approaches to community relations, the chapter ends by suggesting that we take what latter day consociationalists say with a pinch of salt and recall what the pioneer himself said. According to Lijphart, the whole point of consociation is not to weaken communal cleavages but to make society more plural; that is to recognise the cleavages explicitly and to turn them into constructive elements of stable democracy. (Lijphart 1977: 42; see also Porobić 2005). The whole point of this approach to community relations and cultural policy is not reconciliation or to use the current parlance 'good relations', but precisely the production of cultural autonomy and exemplary ethno-national subjects.

These ideas about culture and identity are central to social and political analysis and practice today. So much so that we tend to take them for granted. In Chapter 6 I attempt to shake-up this taken-for-grantedness by tracing the local history of cultural pluralism. Intended as a supplement to the broader intellectual history sketched in Chapter 3, Chapter 6 shows the novelty of the idiom or paradigm of cultural identity when it was introduced to debates in Ireland in the 1970s. John Whyte has described it as a Kuhnian paradigm shift, which is fortuitous because it recalls the well-known comparison by Dreyfus and Rabinow of Kuhn's account of how science develops with Foucault's account of 'normalizing society' more generally. Juxtaposing the scientific and the programmatic – or knowledge and power – in this way is apt in the case of cultural pluralism: this is a concrete example of how a new social science paradigm might acquire a strategic, programmatic, normative, normalising thrust. Cultural pluralism is not just a description of society, it is a prescription as to how it should be.

Notwithstanding the brash confidence with which it is now asserted, there was no unanimity in the 1970s, 1980s, or even early 1990s that the conflict in Northern Ireland was 'about' national identity. The uncertainty was par-ticularly marked in the case of northern protestants who appear to lack any collective project other than the refusal of united Ireland.

Foucault describes government as a rational activity which proceeds by identifying problems and solutions. According to a pluralist political rationality, the Northern Ireland problem was caused by underlying confusions and conflicts of identity (see Whyte 1990). The protestant identity crisis was thought to be particularly acute: in the absence of 'a normal national identity constructed by intellectuals' (O'Dowd 1991: 160) they remained wedded to forms of subjectivity based in an ostentatiously supremacist sectarian popular culture – a residue of colonialism promoted by institutions like the Orange Order. If this is the problem, the construction of ethno-national as against ethno-religious or sectarian forms of subjectivity is a positive solution. As McGarry and O'Leary repeatedly say to critics who complain that the GFA institutionalised sectarianism: 'key provisions in the [Good Friday] Agreement mark it out as a settlement between national communities rather than ethnic or religious communities' (2004: 10).

Turning the ethno-national into a productive aspect of society would appear to make sense. As Lijphart might say to those who complain about the institutionalisation of ethnic divisions: making society more plural is the whole point: it works! In Chapter 7, we explore another context in which the old critique seems inadequate. As part of the common technology of peace, human rights processes are supposed to act as an overarching force that would help bring together the ethnic segments. In neither Northern Ireland or Bosnia-Herzegovina have human rights processes succeeded in this stated purpose. But the problem is not that human rights have become a new terrain upon which old communal conflicts are fought out, which is what the old critique of consociation might lead us to expect. The debates are more complex than that. A feature of both is the reassertion of collective rights over and above the rights of the individual. Principally it is the rights of the ethno-national groups specified in the peace agreements that are reasserted. The only allowance to otherness is to other ethnic minorities. Far from achieving their stated purpose – transcending ethnicity – the human rights processes enacted in Northern Ireland and Bosnia-Herzegovina have inadvertently served to confirm their overweening importance. All difference is welcome so long as it's ethnic!

There is a reluctance, greater in the supposedly more liberal consociation of Northern Ireland than in the more corporate consociation of Bosnia-Herzegovina, to concede anything on the assumption that people born and socialised locally must belong to one of the identity categories specified in the respective peace agreements. These identities perdure and are inescapable. This is to return us to the question with which we started: how so?

Wary of the charge of primordialism, consociationalists respond to this question with a shrug of the realist shoulder: that's how it is and was. In

Chapter 8 we examine this claim in the case of Northern Ireland, where debate has recently turned on the history of socialist politics. Re-examining this history and the emergent literature on 'identity-change', we discover a rich tradition of people who did not conform to the communal scripts and joined together in a movement that occasionally succeeded, if only briefly, in challenging the hegemony of ethnopolitics. Looking at a few such moments, we discover the extent to which ethnic identity is not something that is always already there in a warm primordial fug, but something that was worked at through a variety of practices and institutions, including riots and pogroms and clearances that were not only ethnic, but worked to exclude other kinds of 'misfit'.

From this perspective, the problem with consociational peace agreements is not simply or only or primarily that they recognise and institutionalise particular ethnicities, but that they make ethnicity itself normative and in doing so they close down the space for other ways of being, other ways of being political, other forms of political conflict. As we shall see, the issue is not so much the differences that always exist even within the most apparently closed groups and situations, but the differences, contradictions, and ambiguities that exist within individual subjects.

Approaching conflicts as problems to be solved has generated a shared technology of peace with a demonstrable capacity to facilitate the end of conflict by drawing the protagonists into a power-sharing government. Everybody wins; no one loses. That may be so, but there is still a price. The price of consociational democracy is a foreclosure on other ways of being and ambivalence (Bauman 1991 and 1992).

2 Anthropology, cultural pluralism and consociational theory

Consociational theory has been much refined in recent years. Some of its leading exponents describe themselves as revisionist or liberal consociationalists (McGarry and O'Leary 2004). They pay tribute to Arend Lijphart, the pioneer, but seek to distance themselves from, amongst other things, the frank primordialism of his approach to ethnicity. Much of this refinement to consociational theory is incremental starting in the mid to late 1990s, prompted by the experience of consociational engineering in South Africa, Bosnia Herzegovina and Northern Ireland. There is a tendency for the revisionists to project their revisions backwards in time; so to understand actually existing post-conflict consociations such as Northern Ireland and Bosnia Herzegovina, it is useful to begin with the pioneer, Arend Lijphart.

Northern Ireland, Africa and the consociational pioneers

Consociational theorists were not always so squeamish about primordialism. There is no question that Arend Lijphart, who pioneered the application of consociational theory to conflict resolution in the 1970s operated with a primordial view of what we would now call identity, though the term identity was not so current then as it is now. Lijphart's starting point is theories of pluralism that link 'cultural homogeneity with stability in democracies and heterogeneity with instability' (Lijphart 1975: 99). Drawing on M. G. Smith's anthropological work on West Africa, Lijphart suggests that plural societies 'can be either democratic but unstable or relatively stable but not fully democratic'. He then claims to

> ... have found a third alternative: a culturally divided democracy which is stabilized by an agreement among the leaders of the different subcultures to join in the government of the country. This entails some form of

grand coalition rule and an agreement on an equitable (usually proportional) distribution of appointments, appropriations, etc.

(1975: 99)

In other words power sharing.

Having acknowledged Smith's analysis of pluralism, Lijphart immediately
abandons him for another anthropologist Clifford Geertz.[1] He argues that
communal attachments form the basis for 'non-Western' politics; that 'such
communal attachments are what Geertz calls "primordial" loyalties, which
may be based on language, religion, custom, region, race, or assumed blood
ties' (1975: 17); and that these are foremost among the 'precolonial traditions
that can serve as a firm foundation for consociational democracy'(1977:
166). And not only in 'non-Western' societies, Lijphart also mentions Austria,
Belgium, the Netherlands and Switzerland as consociational democracies:

> The subcultures of the European consociational democracies, which are
> religious and ideological in nature and on which, in two of the countries,
> linguistic divisions are superimposed, may also be regarded as primor-
> dial groups – if one is willing to view ideology as a kind of religion. All
> of these societies, Western and non-Western, will be referred to here as
> plural societies.
>
> (1977: 16)

The early Lijphart was also equally frank about the virtues of communal segregation. This is most evident in his discussion of Northern Ireland. Northern
Ireland was significant to the early development of consociational theory
because it was 'the most unambiguous instance of a plural society . . . in the
Western world' (Lijphart 1977: 134). Better still, from the perspective of
political science, it was a place where something like a consociational agreement – the 'Sunningdale Agreement' of 1973 – had already been tried. The
fact that the power sharing executive established following the Sunningdale
Agreement lasted only five months before collapsing in the face of a strike by
Loyalist workers made Northern Ireland a test case for consociational theory
and policy. In Lijphart's analysis power sharing did not fail because Northern
Irish society was too divided. Paradoxically, sharp cultural divisions were
good for power-sharing:

> Rival subcultures may coexist peacefully if there is little contact between
> them . . . such distinct cleavage [would] promote internal political cohe-
> sion within each subculture and consequently the latitude that leaders

have to strike a political bargain with the leaders of rival subcultures. Such leeway is vital in consociational politics.

(1975: 101)

In the words of Robert Frost's poem, much quoted in Northern Ireland these days (sometimes without the poet's irony): 'good fences make good neighbours'.

In developing his analysis of Northern Ireland as 'the most unambiguous instance of a plural society . . . in the Western world', Lijphart draws heavily on the work of another anthropologist, Rosemary Harris, who did fieldwork in 'Ballybeg' a small town in Northern Ireland in the 1950s:

> Harris reports that in Ballybeg there were few contacts across the religious divide and that when a meeting did occur 'the greatest efforts were made to prevent any controversial topic from being discussed' and she suggests that it was because of the deep religious cleavage that such cross-religious individual contacts were 'particularly 'neighbourly'.

(Lijphart 1975: 101)

It is worth pausing to consider Rosemary Harris because, as will become apparent, her book, *Prejudice and Tolerance in Ulster* (1972, 1986), is foundational to the development of cultural pluralism in Ireland.[2] It certainly made an impact when it was published, not just because of the quality of the fieldwork but also because of its timing when the Troubles were at their fiercest and serious scholarly analyses few. Harris had come to Northern Ireland through chance and family contact. She studied at Queen's University Belfast, and was inspired to conduct fieldwork by the geographer, Estyn Evans, who pioneered ethnology in Northern Ireland. The person who encouraged her to publish the book was the head of the department of anthropology at University College London, where she went to work after leaving Northern Ireland in 1965 – none other than M. G. Smith.

Through her field work, Harris developed a picture of a place divided into 'two basic categories' (1986: xiii), two endogamous communities living in close proximity but remaining strangers to each other. She refuses to call the distinction racial, but she argues that, like race, the religious or ethnic distinction in Northern Ireland had its origins in a system of domination and was made in such 'a wide variety of situations', that it was 'a basic role, like sex or age' (1986: 205–06). The dichotomy was so basic to society as to be impossible to escape, short of leaving Northern Ireland. Given the generalisations made on the basis of Harris's work, we should note that she herself emphasised the importance of locality and the differences between the rural area she studied and the city.

It is in the context of his engagement with the South African transition to democracy that Lijphart becomes more circumspect about the virtues of segregation. Here advocates of consociation ran up against the hostility of those who had already suffered under a system based on ethnic and racial segregation: Lijphart quotes Desmond Tutu: 'we Blacks (most of us) execrate ethnicity with all our being' (Tutu 1984: 121). For the 'consociational engineer' (Lijphart 1995: 280) the problem is a technical one: apartheid involved 'artificially forcing people into racial and ethnic categories [such that] it has become quite unclear what the true dividing lines in the society are'. Lijphart gives two examples of this confusing lack of clarity: English-speaking 'Whites' and 'Coloureds'. The former 'appear to be a residual group rather than a cohesive and self-conscious ethnic segment' (1995: 280–81). With regard to the latter, the confusion was whether they should 'be considered a separate segment' or, since most of them speak Afrikaans and have an Afrikaans cultural background, do they form a single ethnic segment together with White Afrikaners?' (1995: 281). How to decide on the identity of the constituent groups to be included in the power-sharing system and who should be the arbiter?

Lijphart's answer is that the constituent groups to the power-sharing system should be self-determined, and that the way to do this was through elections under some form of proportional representation (PR). Proportional representation is the 'optimal electoral system' for allowing what Lijphart calls segments, ethnic or otherwise, to manifest themselves in the form of political parties in South Africa or any other society, for it allows representation for even very small parties and permits groups to define themselves. He even concedes the possibility that non-ethnic parties – that is, what he calls 'policy-oriented' parties – might emerge. Thus, 'the adoption of PR obviates the need for any prior sorting of divergent claims about the segmental composition of South Africa or any other plural society' (Lijphart 1995: 281) – hence self-determination.

Lijphart does not rule out the pre-determination of groups or a combination of pre-determination and self-determination, but he now prefers the latter. Indeed his discussion of the disadvantages of pre-determination and the advantages of self-determination anticipates some key issues at the heart of this book. Lijphart's examples of power-sharing systems where the constituent groups have been pre-determined are Cyprus (1960 Constitution) and Lebanon. With regard to the former, he notes that recognising the large

Greek and Turkish segments involves potential discrimination against other groups – the examples he gives are Armenians and Maronites. Moreover, he concedes that 'officially registering individuals according to ethnic or other group membership may be controversial, offensive, or even completely unacceptable to many citizens' (1995: 284). Self-determination on the other hand 'gives equal chances not only to all ethnic or other segments . . . but also to groups and individuals who explicitly reject the idea that society should be organised on a segmental basis' (1995: 284). He even quotes with approval a Lebanese author, Theodor Hanf, who argues for the equal recognition of secular groups and individuals alongside the religious communities.

Though Lijphart does not articulate it as such, his 1995 article represents a move in the direction of his 'liberal' critics. The two leading Irish consociational 'revisionists', John McGarry and Brendan O'Leary make the connection. Setting aside their own earlier hostility to 'liberalism', they describe forms of consociation in which the constituent groups are self-determined as 'liberal', and those in which the constituent groups are pre-determined as 'corporate'(2004). The distinguishing features of 'liberal' and corporate consociations are loose, but one of the main ones is that in corporate, pre-determined power-sharing systems there are typically separate electoral registers for each constituent group such that voters can only choose candidates from their own community. On this criterion the Ta'if accords are corporatist and the GFA and the 2005 Iraqi constitution liberal: elections are free in the sense that one can vote for any of the available candidates and parties. The Dayton Accords are corporate because not only did they divide

> Bosnia-Herzegovina into autonomous units, dominated by Bosniaks, Croats, and Serbs, respectively, but also created corporate consociational institutions within Bosnia-Herzegovina's federal government. The latter government is presided over by a rotating presidency based on one Bosniak and one Croat from the Federation of Bosnia-Herzegovina and one Serb from Republika Srpska. The indirectly elected upper chamber of the federal legislature comprises five Bosniaks and five Croats from the Federation of Bosnia-Herzegovina and five Serbs from the National Assembly of Republika Srpska.
>
> (2007: 670)

On the basis of the liberal/corporate distinction McGarry and O'Leary (2007: 677) reject Joe Biden's suggestion, while he was still only a Senator, of Dayton as a model for Iraq, and defend Iraq's 2005 constitution as a liberal consociation.

Returning to the issue of identity we can anticipate that on McGarry and O'Leary's logic liberal consociations will treat identity as 'constructed and malleable', and corporate consociations will treat identity as fixed primordial essence. O'Leary says:

> The distinction between corporate and liberal consociational practice corresponds to that between 'pre-determined' and 'self-determined' identity. The distinction is vital because it is untrue that consociation necessarily privileges, institutionalizes and reinforces prior collective identities. It can do; it need not do so.
>
> (2006: xxv)

Maybe this is the answer to the paradox. Maybe it is the innovation of a form of consociation based on self-determining identity or to put it more succinctly, self-identification, that makes consociation so attractive for the liberal state. Let's see.

Assessing 'liberal' consociation: the illusion of self-identification

In assessing the claims made for what McGarry and O'Leary call 'liberal' consociation, we will focus on Northern Ireland because, Iraq aside, it is the only extant exemplar of what consociationalists themselves designate as a 'liberal' consociation post-conflict. Moreover, the GFA is conveniently explicit about the approach to identity upon which it rests. In item 1(v) and 1 (vi) of the 'Constitutional Issues', the participants to the Agreement

> endorse the commitment made by the British and Irish governments that, in a new British-Irish Agreement replacing the Anglo-Irish Agreement, they will . . .
>
> (v) affirm that whatever choice is freely exercised by a majority of the people of Northern Ireland, the power of the sovereign government with jurisdiction there shall be exercised with rigorous impartiality on behalf of all the people in *the diversity of their identities and traditions* and shall be founded on the principles of full respect for, and equality of, civil, political, social and cultural rights, of freedom from discrimination for all citizens, and of parity of esteem and just and equal treatment for the identity, ethos and aspirations *of both communities*;

(vi) recognise the birthright of all the people of Northern Ireland *to identify themselves and be accepted as Irish or British, or both, as they may so choose,* and accordingly confirm that their right to hold both British and Irish citizenship is accepted by both Governments and would not be affected by any future change in the status of Northern Ireland.

(1998, my emphasis)

These items suggest contradictory assumptions about identity. Item 1(v) seems to suggest an element of what Lijphart and McGarry and O'Leary would call pre-determination. For, while it starts by invoking 'all the people in the diversity of their identities and traditions', it ends by promising, 'parity of esteem' to the identities and ethos of only two communities. But item 1(vi) would appear to confirm what McGarry and O'Leary say about the GFA being liberal and about liberal consociations articulating a view of identity as malleable and open. Some, like Declan Kiberd, would go further. He describes the language of the Agreement as

'poetic' because it offers, a version of multiple identities, of a kind for which no legal language yet exists . . . where is the lawyer who can offer a constitutional definition of identity as open rather than fixed, as a process rather than a conclusion? The . . . Agreement effectively sounds a deathknell for old style Constitutions.

(2000: 628)

Item 1(vi), by allowing for the possibility that people born in Northern Ireland could choose to be Irish or British or both, and be recognised as such, is potentially radical in its implications. It formed the basis for an amendment to the Irish Constitution reaffirming the entitlement to Irish citizenship of anyone born on the island. People born in Northern Ireland were already entitled to Irish citizenship under the Irish constitution, which defined the nation as being coequal with the territory of the island. The Irish Government gave up its claim to the whole territory as a concession to unionists, and it reaffirmed the entitlement to Irish citizenship of anyone born on the island mainly to reassure northern nationalists made anxious by this concession to unionism. Notwithstanding this eminently politic logic, the change to the Irish constitution in line with the GFA does suggest an extraordinary loosening of the relationship between citizenship and national identity.

With the benefit of hindsight, the constitutional changes were not as radical as they seemed. For all the symbolic loosening of the connection between

Irish citizenship and national belonging, the 'people' are still defined as those born here. And in 2004 the Irish Government called a referendum aimed at changing the constitution again to prevent what it called 'citizenship tourism'; that is, women from outside the EU travelling to Ireland to give birth on Irish soil in an attempt to secure citizenship. The referendum, said the government, was merely a matter of closing an unfortunate 'loophole' created in a heroic dash to secure peace. But it was more than that. According to the Minister for Justice, the referendum was also about reasserting an intimate connection between citizenship, national identity and political community, or 'the essence of the intertwined concepts of citizenship and nationality' as the Minister called it (see Finlay 2004). But if this were the whole truth of the matter, the Government would have done something about the 'Irish Granny rule', according to which the children and grandchildren of Irish citizens living abroad, including hundreds of thousands of people who have no other connection to the island nor any desire to live here, have the right to claim Irish citizenship. Leaving 'the Irish Granny rule' intact gives substance to the allegation that the 2004 referendum was racist (Peter Finlay 2004). We should also note that the apparently unilateral nature of the Irish government's action in effectively altering the terms of the GFA dismayed some of the local parties to the Agreement. The Irish government's response – that it had already confirmed with the British Government that the referendum was not a breach of the Agreement – tells us something about the Agreement's top-down nature.

Priding themselves on their realism, McGarry and O'Leary avoid extravagant claims and offer a more sober assessment of the GFA than Kiberd. To their credit they confront head-on one of its most glaringly corporatist features; that is the requirement that members of the local power sharing assembly set up under the agreement register as 'unionists', 'nationalist' or 'others':

> This was enacted to provide a veto for the nationalist minority (and a future unionist minority, should one materialize): the passage of important measures requires the support of at least forty per cent of both registered nationalist[s] and unionists. One effect of this is [t]hat it pr[i]vileges nationalist and unionist over 'others'. Arguably it creates a minor incentive for voters to support nationalist or unionists, or for elected members to register as nationalists or unionists, as members of these groups will count more than 'others'. It also has the effect of pre-determining, in advance of election results, that nationalists and unionists are to be better protected than 'others'.
>
> (McGarry 2001: 123)

But they stress once again that such corporate mechanisms are not 'intrinsic to consociational design' (McGarry and O'Leary 2004: 33). They lay out alternative arrangements which would have had the same effect, and claim that it was the local political parties who spoilt the sleek liberal mechanism, converging on corporatism, albeit for understandable reasons: 'genuine existential anxieties about the security of the communities they represent' (2004: 33). Note the use of the word 'existential' here, we will return to this again.

For the moment allow me to give you a flavour of what the requirement to register an identity involves and what it implies about identity. There were two parties that organised on a cross community basis in the first Assembly convened after elections held in 1998: the liberal Alliance Party and the Women's Coalition. Alliance secured six seats and the Women's Coalition two. MLAs from both parties were forced to change their identification on a number of occasions. The latter case is particularly instructive. The Coalition was formed in 1996 to ensure that Northern Ireland's future would not be negotiated solely by men. The Coalition didn't pretend that women weren't divided by constitutional politics. Among its founding members were unionists and nationalists as well as 'others'. But it also argued that, 'even for unionists and nationalists, these are not the only differences that matter, and that the way they matter is not immutable' (Whitaker 2004: 160). Reflecting the fact that it included British-identified unionists and Irish-identified nationalists, as well as people who would not be described by either label, the two Women's Coalition MLAs initially registered as 'Nationalist/Unionist/Other Other' and 'Unionist/Nationalist/Other Other', respectively. Having been informed that these identities were ambiguous and unacceptable, the two MLAs amended their designations to 'inclusive other'.

They, alongside the Alliance MLAs, were required to re-designate for a second time in November 2001. First Minister David Trimble had resigned to put pressure on the republican movement to decommission weapons. When the republicans responded, Trimble sought reinstatement as First Minister. He was opposed by the Democratic Unionist Party. The votes of the two Women's Coalition MLAs were vital to save the Agreement, but for these votes to be counted valid the MLAs were required to re-designate as 'Nationalist' or 'Unionist'. Whatever item 1(vi) of the Agreement might say about the 'birth-right of all the people of Northern Ireland to identify themselves as Irish or British or both', the designation rules 'assume that political representatives have a substantive identity: unionist or nationalist. Others are defined purely in negative terms; all that matters is what they are not' (Whitaker 2004: 170). Or, to use Rosemary Harris's language: the designation rules in the GFA suggest that for everyone socialised in Northern Ireland ethnicity is a 'basic' identity.

McGarry and O'Leary present this as an unfortunate lapse to corporatism, a concession to some of the local political parties involved in the peace negotiation, but not intrinsic to consociational design. And beyond the identity-designation rules in Assembly, they argue that corporate tendencies are offset by liberal measures. 'The agreement not only stresses equality ("parity of esteem") between nationalist and unionists, it also offers protection to individuals, including those who regard themselves as neither unionist nor nationalist' (McGarry 2001: 122). McGarry mentions the statutory obligation on public authorities 'to promote equality of opportunity in relation to religion, and political opinion, gender; race; disability; marital status; dependents; and sexual orientation'. He also mentions the short-lived Civic Forum which was supposed to provide an opportunity for those who do not feel represented by conventional political parties to have their voices heard.

But the key protection was supposed to be provided by the human rights provisions of the Agreement. The GFA entrenches the European Convention on Human Rights in Northern Ireland law, and the Agreement makes provision for a Northern Ireland Human Rights Commission (NIHRC) charged with advising the Secretary of State on the development of a Bill of Rights to supplement the provisions of the European Convention for Human Rights (ECHR). According to the GFA, any additional rights were 'to reflect the particular circumstances of Northern Ireland . . . the principles of mutual respect for the identity and ethos of both communities and parity of esteem' (letter from the Secretary of State for Northern Ireland to the NIHRC 24 March 1999, quoted in NIHRC 10 December 2008, p. 8). The proposed Bill of Rights has proved so contentious that after the resignations of several commissioners, the reappointment of the commission and two drafts of the proposed Bill of Rights, there is still no agreement.

Protracted debate and apparent failure would appear to be the sad fate of the human rights provisions of peace agreements. We will return in Chapter 7 to the human rights fallout from the GFA and the Dayton Accords. But to sustain the argument of this chapter and the next, it is useful for the reader to be aware of some of the issues, at least as they manifested themselves in the skirmishing around the first attempt to draft a Bill of Rights in Northern Ireland.

The first Human Rights Commission set up after the signing of the agreement was divided from the outset between those commissioners who wanted the Bill of Rights to stick with the old liberal convention according to which rights accrue to humans as individuals and those commissioners who thought the Bill of Rights should more strongly reflect the principle of parity of esteem for the 'two communities' fore-grounded in the GFA. According to Robin Wilson, a critic of consociation who was also a member of the Bill of Rights Culture and Identity Working Group, the EHCR would imply recognition of those who chose '*not* to be treated as a member of what might be perceived to be their national, ethnic, religious or linguistic community', while an emphasis on parity of esteem 'would involve deleting the right-of-exit clause' (Wilson 2003: 11, my emphasis; see also Wilson 11 January 2001).

In the broader debate, those who supported the right of exit did so in the name of 'self-identification':

> Northern Ireland is already more diverse than the 'two communities' approach would suggest . . . This 'two communities' or 'both communities' language fails to acknowledge that a significant number of people cannot be labeled as Unionists or Nationalists, protestants or Catholics. Some people come from mixed marriages, are part of ethnic minorities, or choose not be described in such terms, preferring a more multicultural and pluralist self-identification.

> (Alliance Party 2001)

Those who opposed a right of exit or right to self-identification did not confine themselves to asserting the priority of parity of esteem. They also articulated an anxiety that a right of exit would put at risk procedures for monitoring the composition of job applicants and workforces, for these monitoring procedures have 'a fall back provision allowing designation of individuals into a community without their consent' (McCrudden 2009: 8). This fall back provision will be detailed in Chapter 4. For the moment we should simply note that those opposed to a right of exit won, and the most recent draft Bill of Rights does not allow for a right of exit from community.

This reluctance to allow a right of exit is extraordinary. A right to exit is the bottom line for even the most ardent advocates of group rights (e.g. see Kymlicka 1995: 14). In part, it might be understood in terms of the strength of feeling around fair employment legislation arising from the history of systematic discrimination against Catholics. But there is something else to keep in mind. One consociational theorist who was also an architect of the fair employment legislation, Christopher McCrudden, points out that the employment monitoring procedures and the designation rules in the assembly are linked in that 'both rely to some extent on using group identity as an important element in the way they are operationalized' (2007: 317). The employment monitoring procedures precede and are used retrospectively to support the designation rules in the legislature, but the first did not lead to the second in any linear way. We will return to this point in Chapter 9, here I want to resist imputing a connection between the two other than that both are consistent with the underlying pluralist rationality as elaborated by Rosemary Harris and taken-up by Lijphart: in Northern Ireland: ethnicity is as 'basic' to one's identity as sex.

The apparent absence of a 'right to exit' in post-Agreement Northern Ireland returns us to the very anxiety that Lijphart sought to avoid through invoking the self-determination of the constituent groups to a power-sharing system: who is it that gets to decide what the relevant groups are and, more to the point, 'who belongs to which group'? (Kymlicka 1995: 16).

Conclusion

Revisionist consociationalists are keen to refute the charge that the theory and practice they espouse rests on a view of identity as a primordial essence. To this end McGarry and O'Leary develop Lijphart's distinction between a type of consociation in which the constituent groups to the power-sharing arrangement are pre-determined, and a type in which they are self-determined. The former type is called corporate consociation, the latter liberal. McGarry and O'Leary concede that corporate, pre-determined consociations imply the reductiveness typical of primordialism, but insist that liberal, self-determined ones clearly do not. The distinction is, 'vital because it is untrue that consociation necessarily privileges, institutionalizes and reinforces prior collective identities. It can do; it need not do so' (O'Leary 2006: xxv). Northern Ireland is particularly important to this argument because the GFA is the best example of actually existing liberal consociation.

Unfortunately, when one looks at the outworking of certain key aspects of the Agreement, the room for self-determination or self-identification seems to be severely curtailed or threatened. Most obvious is the requirement that elected members of the legislature established by the agreement must designate an identity. But even measures that appear to allow or facilitate a measure of self-determination – the provision for a Bill of Rights and citizenship – do not measure up.

Having asserted that the GFA is a liberal consociation, McGarry and O'Leary are scrupulous in documenting how far it falls short. As if exhausted by the effort McGarry eventually concedes that constituent groups to power-sharing in Northern Ireland are 'pre-determined' and falls back on the assertion that 'in this case, the pre-determined groups have constituted almost all of the electorate for the past century' (2001: 123; see also McGarry and O'Leary 2004: 19). In other words, the GFA may institutionalise ethnic or sectarian politics but it was always thus.

We will examine this assertion in Chapter 8, but we should note here that McGarry and O'Leary offer no empirical elaboration of the 100-year continuity in identity politics (except perhaps to disparage political traditions and parties that do not conform to their binary teleology) nor do they theorise it. Writing in 1995, they veer close to the idea that ethnicity is the ubiquitous product of an innate need to belong:

> Ethnic communities are perceived kinship groups. Their members share a subjective belief in their common ancestry . . . The sense which such communities have of real or imagined kinship may explain the ubiquity of ethno-nationalism – it satisfies the human need to belong, to feel 'at home', in an otherwise atomistic world. Since an ethno-national group regards itself as a large extended family, its members regard an attack on one as an attack on all. . . .
>
> (1995: 354–55)

More recently they simply assert, 'there is a major difference between thinking that identities are durable and maintaining they are immutably primordial' (2004: 32). Semantics aside, what precisely is the difference?

Attempting to answer such questions is crucial to the notion of 'liberal' consociation, and to the broader existential and political questions that revisionist consociationalists raise, yet, having disavowed primordialism, they give us little idea of their thinking.[3]

3 Essentialism and the reconciliation of the liberal state to ethnicity

Consociationalists have responded to the 'liberal' critique by distinguishing liberal and corporate forms. In the former the participating groups are said to be self-determined; in the latter pre-determined. In line with this, consociational revisionists claim that there is a difference between accepting the fact that identities are durable but malleable constructs and believing them to be an unchanging primordial inheritance. None of these distinctions are as stable as consociationalists would like to believe. Looking at the best example of actually existing liberal consociation – the GFA – we saw that the scope for self-determination is institutionally severely circumscribed. Following Brubaker and Cooper, I would also wish to question the viability of the analytical distinction between a constructivist and primordial or essentialist understanding of identity. Given the unpalatable associations of essentialism, 'academic correctness' (2000: 6) requires lip service to constructivism, but when it comes down to it, there is little to choose because either way ethnic identity is taken for granted as something that 'is always already "there" as something that individuals and groups "have"' (2000: 28).

To simply assert that ethnic identities are durable and that we must face up to their enduring reality without broaching what it is that makes them durable is to evade much scholarly work and debate.[1] For me the most interesting evasion is the evasion of the literature on the relationship between culture and identity. Reading the work of consociational revisionists like McGarry and O'Leary the evasion seems more like a disavowal, albeit with lapses.

As articulated by Arend Lijphart, cultural recognition and autonomy is one of the four principles of consociationalism. The idea is that democracy is difficult without fellow-feeling and shared values. Unnerved perhaps by the accusation of primordialism, McGarry and O'Leary distance themselves from this aspect of Lijphart's theory (see 2009: 28). McGarry makes a sharp distinction between ethno-national communities and 'mere cultural communities'

(2004: 324). The latter can be addressed through multiculturalism; the former require recognition not of their culture but of their political aspirations.

The sharp distinction revisionists seek to maintain between consociation and multiculturalism would be lost on some of the key parties to and supporters of the GFA, notably the President of Ireland Mary McAleese (see McAleese 2001) and former Taoiseach (Prime Minister), Bertie Ahern (see Ahern 2000). And it is not consistently maintained; for example McGarry and O'Leary (2009: 16) describe a continuum of institutional form and there are lapses to a more Lijphartian position on cultural or segmental autonomy.

This disavowal of the 'merely' cultural by Lijphart's heirs, if not the man himself, inhibits our understanding of two things: first, of ethno-national identity and its apparent staying power; second, of how the liberal state reconciles itself to a form of conflict resolution that incentivises some very illiberal practices and subjects or identities. The rhetorical distancing of consociation from multiculturalism is particularly unfortunate in the latter regard, for it obscures the extent to which both draw their legitimacy from a cultural pluralism or politics of recognition rooted in German philosophy filtered though American anthropology.

The 'old' idea of culture and the politics of recognition

The political philosophers who have developed a liberal approach to multiculturalism and cultural recognition – Will Kymlicka and Charles Taylor – are a little more upfront in this regard. In the introduction to an edited collection that also features an article by Lijphart, Kymlicka follows Avishai Margalit and Joseph Raz in arguing that membership of what they call a 'pervasive culture' is crucial not only to identity but to well-being:

cultural membership provides people with meaningful choices about how to lead their lives . . . hence if a culture is *decaying or discriminated against*, 'the options and opportunities open to its members will shrink, become less attractive, and their pursuit less likely to be successful . . .' of course the members of a *decaying* culture could integrate into another culture but Margalit and Raz argue that this is difficult . . . because of the role of culture in peoples' self-identity . . . Cultural identity provides an 'anchor for a [peoples'] self identification and the safety of effortless secure belonging'. But this in turn means that people's self-respect is bound up with the esteem in with their *national* group is held. If a culture is not generally respected then the dignity and self-respect of its members will also be threatened.

(1995: 7, my emphasis)

Being possessed of a group culture is crucial to the dignity of the individual. One of the notable things about this quote is that it starts by referring to 'decaying culture' – one thinks of indigenous peoples facing cultural extinction – and ends by referring to 'national' groups. Kymlicka's elision of the differences between these various – very different – kinds of group is suggestive anthropological ignorance. Margalit and Raz's discussion of 'pervasive cultures' and 'encompassing groups' is conducted at an abstract level without references and bibliography, but the concept of culture with which they are working would appear to be what I, following Susan Wright (1998), will call the 'old' anthropological concept of culture. The '"old" idea of culture' is an artefact from the age of imperialism, and is associated with a relativistic view of a world made up of discrete peoples each with their own distinct way of life. In this worldview, cultures are spatially located, closed and homogeneous: inherited meanings are shared equally by all the members of the culture. As Scott has pointed out, 'culture in political theory remains oddly untheorized, oddly unhistoricized; it is merely and fundamentally there, like a non ideological background, or a natural horizon' (2003: 113).

The evocation of a heritable sameness and homogeneity is what is conventionally understood when the term 'essentialism' or 'primordialism' is used, and it is this that licences the corporatist idiom in which the one can stand for the group. However, the old idea of culture also has a psychological dimension. As Craig Calhoun (1997) argues essentialism refers not just to the reduction of diversity in a population to some shared set of primordial inherited characteristics: '[t]wo further guiding assumptions in much modern thinking on matters of identity are that individuals ideally ought to achieve maximally integrated identities, and that to do so they need to inhabit self-consistent, unitary cultures or life-worlds' (1997: 18–19). Kymlicka and Margalit and Raz make explicit the strong psychological undertow to primordialism, but it remains implicit in consociational theory.

The potent import of the psychologism implicit in the old idea of culture finds what is still its most eloquent expression in the famous response of the Executive Board of the American Anthropological Association to the Universal Declaration of Human Rights, drafted in 1947, and adopted by the United Nations General Assembly in 1948. Consistent with the liberal tradition, the Declaration defined rights as belonging to individuals. Against this, the Association's Executive Board argued that,

The individual realizes his personality through his culture, hence a respect for individual differences entails a respect for cultural differences ... There can be no individual freedom, that is, when the group with which the individual identifies is not free. There can be no full development of the individual personality as long as the individual is told, by men who have the power to enforce their commands, that the way of life of his group is inferior to that of those who wield the power.

(1947: 541)

Generalising the old idea of culture from small and threatened groups to the nation

The people involved in drafting this statement, Melville Herskovits for example, had in mind 'the small communities in colonized regions, such as Africa and the Caribbean' that they had studied as anthropologists. Its broader applicability was queried at the time by other renowned anthropologists such as Julian Steward (Merry 2003: 57). The question is: how was this view of the relationship between cultural and individual identity generalised such that Kymlicka can extend it from the small, threatened indigenous communities that the American Anthropological Association had in mind to large national groups? The question is all the more pertinent because this view of culture has its origins in an intellectual tradition that was hostile to the universalism upon which human rights were originally based: the old anthropological concept of culture was developed by the father of American anthropology, Franz Boas, but he got it from Johanne Gottfried Herder for whom it was a rejection of Enlightenment Humanism.

In seeking to explain how the American Anthropological Association's view of culture and personality was generalised from the kinds of communities studied by anthropologists in the colonial world there are two important trajectories, both forged during and after the Second World War. One is the United Nations Educational, Scientific and Cultural Organisation (UNESCO). UNESCO's founding conference in London in 1945 was initially premised on the idea that to ensure that fascism could never rise again all that was required was a reassertion of Enlightenment verities about the free individual. One of the speakers was the anthropologist Claude Levi-Strauss who argued that what Europe had to escape wasn't only fascism but also colonialism, and with this in mind he nudged the conference away from Enlightenment universalism in the direction of cultural relativism. The history of UNESCO is well known (e.g. see Wright 1998 and Eriksen 2001), and, for reasons that will become apparent, I would prefer to highlight the second trajectory, mapped by Phillip Gleason (1983).

Gleason stresses the role of Boas' students who formed the culture and personality school of anthropology, and, even more, their psychological associate Erik Erikson. Erikson, a refugee from Nazi Germany, worked with Margaret Mead and others in national character studies that aimed to help the war effort and involving applying the 'old' idea to societies and phenomena well beyond the small, threatened communities usually studied by anthropologists. Erikson conducted a study which attempted to explain why German young people had gravitated to Hitler. 'He suggested that Hitler had been successful "in winning the loyalty of German youth by embodying in himself the anxieties and fantasies of a generation that, after the humiliation of WWI had experienced cultural crisis and economic collapse"' (Gleason 1983: 925). The most famous example of this kind of work is that carried out by Ruth Benedict under the auspices of the Office of War Information. Her study of Japan, *The Chrysanthemum and the Sword* (1946), sought to make Japanese culture more intelligible to American administrators responsible for running the country in the aftermath of the War.

In its orientation and approach, the culture and personality school prefigures subsequent deployments of the culture concept in the management of diversity (multiculturalism) and conflict.[2] The innovation of the culture and personality school is not so much putting knowledge at the service of the state in wartime, that is familiar enough, it is in following through the methodological innovations made possible by applying the old idea of culture to whole nation states. What this enables is a reduction of personal identities to national cultures such that individual behaviour and attitudes can be read-off from 'the culture'. Past actions could be interpreted and future actions anticipated without the social scientist ever having to visit the country: remotely, or 'at a distance' as the anthropologists employed by the Unites States Office of War Information put it. The cultural and personality school focused on the garnering of knowledge about culture with a view to controlling a national population (c.f. Price 2008: 40).

Erikson's psychology is crucial here. As one would expect of a Freudian psychologist, Erikson regarded personal identity as something internal that persists even as the individual changes in response to the developmental tasks associated with biological maturation and the role-requirements associated with his or her cultural milieu. Erikson coined the term, 'identity crisis' to describe the 'climactic turning point in this process ... [which] usually occurs in adolescence, but can also be precipitated by unusual difficulties further along in the life-cycle (Gleason 1983: 914). Change and crisis notwithstanding, an individual's identity is at bottom an accrued confidence in the inner sameness and continuity of his/her own being. For Erikson, an exponent of the democratic project of American ego psychology and a firm believer in the ideal of the well-balanced personal identity, this inner sameness and continuity is something to be valued and nurtured. Despite his emphasis on identity as something interior to the individual, Erikson regarded identity as inextricably bound up with the communal culture. In an abidingly influential formulation he reduces individual identity to communal identity: identity as 'a process located in the core of the individual and yet also in the core of his communal culture, a process which establishes . . . the identity of those identities' (Erikson 1968: 22). As Gleason points out, the linkage that Erikson implies between personal identity and an inherited communal culture makes plausible,

> the argument that cultures – especially minority ethnic cultures – require some sort of official recognition if the self-esteem of individuals is not to suffer damage. The respect for the dignity of the individual demanded by democratic ideology is thereby extended to cover ethnic cultures that sustain the sense of personal self worth.
>
> (Gleason 1983: 921)

Thus are liberals and democrats reconciled with ethnicity and cultural rights and the way is clear for the generalisation of these ideas beyond oppressed minorities and indigenous peoples threatened with cultural extinction.

Consociationalism, parity of esteem and the notion of cultural self-determination

Consociationalists may not be as explicit as Will Kymlicka (1995), Charles Taylor (1994) and the others, but cultural recognition is clearly central to their concerns. Thus Lijphart does not speak of cultural rights, he speaks of 'segmental autonomy', but it amounts to the same thing. According to the consociational principle of segmental autonomy, 'any cultural group that wishes to have internal autonomy can be given the *right* to establish a "cultural council," a publicly *recognized* body equivalent to a state in a federation' (1995: 282, my emphasis). The main task of such 'cultural councils' is the 'administration of schools for those who wish to receive an education according to the group's linguistic and cultural traditions' (1995: 282), but it might also organise other cultural institutions such as libraries and theatres. The prime example is the familiar one: Belgium. Lijphart admits that the cultural councils established for the Dutch, French and German communities in Belgium were pre-determined, but presumably with liberal sensibilities in mind, Lijphart stresses cultural autonomy as a self-determining process. He gives the example of a law of cultural autonomy enacted by the Estonian government in 1925, under which ethnic minorities 'with more than 3,000 formally registered members had the right to establish autonomous institutions under the authority of a cultural council elected by the minority' (1995: 283). German and Jewish minorities responded by setting up their own autonomous cultural authorities.

In the debate on the GFA, McGarry and O'Leary have responded to complaints about their primordialism by distancing themselves from notions of culture and cultural autonomy. They emphasise a supposed difference between the institutional recognition of national identity and cultural recognition (McGarry 2001: 127). There is the occasional lapse; for example, when McGarry and O'Leary impute 'existential anxieties' to the local parties who they hold responsible for introducing corporatist elements to the GFA (McGarry and O'Leary 2004: 33).

In view of this denial, it is important to trace the formal development of the notion of parity of esteem, which is GFA parlance for cultural recognition. In doing so, I wish to show two things. One is that cultural recognition is central to the consociational agreement that is the GFA. The other is that it was not introduced at the last minute by local parties suffering existential angst about the cultural survival of their respective groups.

The first published expression of the term 'parity of esteem' is to be found in a report (see Hennessey and Wilson 1997) prepared for the Secretary of State for Northern Ireland by the Standing Advisory Commission on Human Rights (SACHR 1990), the predecessor of the Northern Ireland Human Rights Commission. The report concludes,

> that it would be desirable to include in a new Northern Ireland Constitution Act a general statement recognising the existence of the two main sections of the community in Northern Ireland and imposing a duty on Government and other public authorities and bodies to ensure that their functions are carried out in such a way as to ensure that members of both main sections of the community are granted *equality of treatment and esteem.*
>
> (1990: 91, my emphasis)

From the vantage point of today, when one no longer has a right of exit from the community into which one was born, SACHR's consideration of 'granting some form of formal constitutional or legislative recognition of the existence of two major sections of the community in Northern Ireland' (1990: 76) seems remarkably tentative. SACHR recognise that there is a difference of opinion among 'human rights lawyers' on the relationship between individual and group rights but eschews the debate because it 'does not think it appropriate to express a view on theoretical and philosophical issues of this kind' (1990: 77).

Rather than discuss the theoretical and philosophical issues, the report proceeds by means of legal precedents (Belgium – the consociational favourite – features) and practical examples. Notable here is its attempt to salvage the notion of segregated education from the ignominy of the famous *Brown versus Board of Education* case (1954). Brown vs Board of Education was a landmark decision by the United States Supreme Court, which outlawed racial segregation in public education. It ruled that separate but equal provision in public education could not provide African-Americans with the same standard of education as White Americans. The decision galvanised the Civil Rights Movement. SACHR admits that there are problems with the provision of 'separate but equal' schools for children from such communities; but argues that such provision is 'an acceptable way of pursuing the objective of full equality of treatment and esteem' so long as the facilities are genuinely equal, and with 'two provisos' (1990: 79). The main proviso is that 'there should be no imposed segregation and no unreasonable curtailment of the rights of those who wish to live and work in or work towards an integrated or homogeneous society' (1990: 79–80). Falling back on the pious optimism of what McGarry calls 'the consociational paradox' (2001: 124), the SACHR report claims that a policy of equality of esteem would 'not necessarily result in an increase in . . . divisions and tensions',

> and may also give the members and leaders of the communities involved sufficient reassurance and confidence that their fundamental interests and *values* will not be ignored or overruled to facilitate or encourage the compromises necessary to achieve . . . joint participation in the structures of government.
>
> (1990: 87, my emphasis)

Tentative and unsure of the intellectual ground, SACHR gives the Anglo-Irish Agreement of 1987 as the ultimate warrant for parity of esteem. An international agreement between the British and Irish Governments registered with the United Nations, the Anglo-Irish Agreement obliged the British Government to introduce 'measures to recognise and accommodate the rights and identities of the two traditions in Northern Ireland, to protect human rights and to prevent discrimination' (1990: 84). SACHR notes that on the back of the Anglo-Irish Agreement the government had 'established a Community Relations Council whose functions include the fostering of both *traditions* within Northern Ireland' (1990: 89, my emphasis).

Following the Anglo-Irish Agreement – that is before what became known as the peace process began – huge resources were invested in community relations and 'cultural traditions' work. Some of this involved cross community contact, but as we shall discuss in Chapter 5, there was and is a lot of what has come to be known as 'single-identity' work aimed at bolstering the self-esteem of members of each community whether as a prelude to cross community contact or not.

The SACHR report acknowledges the work of the Community Relations Council, but it did not consider it to be sufficient: there were still outstanding matters to be dealt with relating to the Irish language and education, and

> there is no constitutional . . . guarantee that either under continuing direct rule [from Britain] or in the event of the devolution of powers on such matters to a Northern Ireland Assembly . . . objectionable measures might not be enacted in the future.
>
> (1990: 89–90)

Although the focus is on the nationalist minority, the SACHR report argues that,

> similar considerations apply in respect of the protection of the unionist and British *tradition* in parts of Northern Ireland where nationalists are in control or more generally if the government of Northern Ireland were to be controlled by parties more interested in or committed to the nationalist or Irish *tradition*.
>
> (1990: 90, my emphasis)

Clearly, there is more going on here than a pragmatic recognition of the existence of two 'communities', 'traditions', or 'sections': there is an assumption that they each have a special 'cultural heritage' (1990: 79) which demands expression and recognition here, now and in perpetuity such that prophylactic measures are required in the event of a variety of possible political outcomes. One might even get the impression that culture or ethnicity is prior to and pre-empts politics.

Conclusion

In response to the allegation that consociationalism is primordialist and freezes antagonistic identities, consociational revisionists elaborate (improvise might be a better word) a distinction between liberal and corporate consociation. They concede that corporate consociations can reasonably be characterised as primordialist because the constituent groups to the power-sharing arrangement are pre-determined, but in liberal consociations, the constituent groups are self-determined, with identities that are understood as contingent and constructed. This distinction has been further elaborated by McGarry and O'Leary in their intervention to the debate about Iraq's constitution (2007). Here they reject those who advocate a corporatist approach based on the Dayton accords.

The GFA remains the best example of an actually existing liberal consociational agreement. Unfortunately, post-conflict Northern Ireland does not quite measure up. In the period before the signing of the GFA, there may have been formal political self-determination – the elections held were by proportional representation and were free in the sense that one was not required to vote for a particular list of candidates or parties – but there was a process of cultural pre-determination sponsored by the British and Irish States and sanctioned by an international agreement between them, the Anglo-Irish Agreement of 1987.

Consociationalists present themselves as pragmatic political realists who recognise that while identities are not immutable essences, ethnicity is nevertheless a durable force to be reckoned with. In their desire to avoid the taint of primordialism, they fail to appreciate that it is precisely essentialism that enables the liberal state to embrace ethnicity. Essentialism implies individual identity is so bound up with collective cultural identity that if the latter is not recognised our self-esteem and dignity as individuals will suffer: 'the respect for the dignity of the individual demanded by democratic ideology is thereby extended to cover ethnic cultures that sustain the sense of personal self worth' (Gleason 1983: 921). On this logic, ethnicity is not merely a force to be reckoned with; it is a positive good! As we shall see, the operationalisation of this idea is central to efficacy of consociational peace agreements.

The Standing Advisory Commission on Human Rights who introduced the notion of 'equality of esteem' did so tentatively and with due regard for those who might not want to live in a segregated society. What was introduced in 1990 with such circumspection has become increasingly normative. Thus, the argument between those human rights commissioners who wanted the proposed Bill of Rights to follow the logic of parity of esteem and those commissioners who worried that this would mean denying an individual's right to exit from his/her community of origin is settled in favour of the former:

> as any good liberal should know . . . communal life is as central a part of personal autonomy as anything else. Much contemporary liberal thinking recognises the value of communal and cultural life to the individual.

> (Harvey 2003: 9)

All this with the imprimatur of social science: in the new Northern Ireland there are PhDs awarded to research showing that 'segregation may be beneficial to the psychological well-being of individuals in segregated cultures, particularly when it favours the individuals' ethnic group' (University of Ulster Press Release, 1 July 2008).

4 Is ethnopolitics a form of biopolitics?

According to the theory of identity that renders cultural autonomy palatable to the liberal state, cultures – especially minority ethnic cultures – require some sort of official recognition if the self-esteem of individuals is not to suffer damage. 'As Gleason (1983) suggests: the individual realises his/her personality through his/her culture, therefore a respect for individual differences entails a respect for cultural differences.' There are many problems with this argument, and we will touch on some of them later in the book, but I do not wish to deny those whose self-understanding depends on this view of their culture and identity (see Gutman 1994 and Wren 2002). What I want to develop here is a different argument: that the problem with consociation is less the fact that it valorises particular ethno-national traditions, but that it valorises ethnicity per se and makes it normative, such that the space for other ways of being and other forms of politics is diminished. To take a short cut into this argument, let me invoke the work of Asim Mujkic, a Bosnian critic of the Dayton Accords:

> Due to her or his marginalized and discriminated-against position under the [Dayton] Constitution, a Bosnian citizen is valuable only as a member of an ethnic group. He or she, according to ethnopolitical expectations, has two purposes in his or her individual life: a reproductive purpose (to increase the biological mass of the collective) and a pseudopolitical purpose (to vote for 'his or her kin' in elections). Both of these functions or purposes are deeply biological. In the first case, this is obvious. The second presupposes that a vote for the representative of a person's kinship group is a precondition both for the existence of the group and for that of the individual. In other words, you don't vote for lower taxes, ecological laws, and the like; rather, you vote for your own survival (every four years or so). So each and every election is described during the

campaign as 'decisive,' 'crucial', a 'matter of life or death'. . . taking part in politics takes the form of obeying a biological obligation. In this sense, ethnopolitics is a form of biopolitics. *The notion of the individual citizen, abstracted from his ethnic and religious kinship, is viewed as subversive. It is thought of as a despicable form of atheism, moral corruption, decadence, and rebellion.*

(2007: 119, my emphasis)

When I say that the problem with consociational arrangements is that they make ethnicity normative, this is what I mean – other ways of being come to be seen as flawed or dubious: worthy of disparagement and subject to sanction.

According to the argument that I wish to develop in the course of this book, the normalisation of ethnicity is both crucial to the efficacy of consociational agreements and a damaging weakness. We already have an inkling of this from Chapter 2, where we noted the rules requiring members of the legislature established under the GFA to designate themselves as unionist or nationalist or other. And there are the difficulties created for the human rights provisions of the GFA by employment monitoring legislation that allows employees and job applicants to be designated into a community against their wishes. We will discuss the latter later in this chapter. For the moment I want to follow through on Mujkic's suggestion that 'ethnopolitics is a form of biopolitics', for this provides another important route into my argument.

Biopolitics, race science and cultural essentialism

'Biopolitics', together with another neologism, 'biopower', are part of Foucault's analysis of the development of sovereignty from feudal forms in the Middle Ages, when the sovereign's power rested on the right to kill or refrain from killing, to modern liberal forms that rest less on established authority than on the power to foster and invest life: 'methods of power and knowledge assumed responsibility for the life process and undertook to control and modify them' (Foucault 1980: 142). Foucault traces the emergence of biopower/biopolitics from the seventeenth century, focusing on the regulation of sex and sexuality as pivotal in the development of 'the entire political technology of life' at the level of the population and of the individual (1980: 145). Departing from Weber's famous definition of a state, which emphasises its monopoly of the means of physical coercion, Foucault is describing forms of power that depend on the social or cultural norm as part of what he subsequently calls 'governmental rationality' or 'governmentality':

Another consequence of this development of bio-power was the growing importance assumed by the action of the norm, at the expense of the juridical system of the law. Law cannot help but be armed, and its arm, par excellence, is death; to those that transgress it, it replies, at least as last resort, with that absolute menace . . . But a power whose task is to take charge of life needs continuous regulatory and corrective mechanisms. It is no longer a matter of bringing death into play in the field of sovereignty, but of distributing the living in the domain of value and utility. Such a power has to qualify, measure, appraise, and heirarchize, rather than display itself in its murderous splendour . . . it effects distributions around the norm.

(Foucault 1980: 144)

So far so good: Mujkic's equation – ethnopolitics equals biopolitics – would appear to be consistent with our suggestion that the rationale of forms of post-conflict government influenced by consociationalism is to normalise ethnicity. However we need to proceed carefully. Foucault's development of the notions of biopolitics, biopower and the related notion of 'governmentality' is hardly systematic or sustained, and, perhaps because of this, these notions have sometimes been burdened with a weight of historical generalisation that they cannot bear (Rabinow and Rose 2003). The Serbian–Bosnian and other ethnic conflicts present us with a particular dilemma. For Foucault, the emergence of biopower is a key part of the transition to government as a rational activity based on scientific knowledge about the health and welfare of the population and the individual. In contrast, as Valverde (2007) points out, the Serbian–Bosnian conflict appears to hark back to what Foucault calls the 'race wars' of the Middle Ages, with their pre-scientific discourse of 'blood and honour'. On this logic, to describe ethnopolitics as a form of biopolitics appears to be stretch.

This dilemma links to another one. Foucault's argument that modern forms of government came to rely more on an enabling power over life and less on the power of death and coercion seems to be contradicted by a history that shows that 'wars were never as bloody as they have been since the nineteenth century . . . never before did regimes visit such holocausts on their own populations' (1980: 136–37). Foucault confronts this apparent contradiction head-on: it is precisely because states have become 'managers of life and survival, of bodies and the race' that 'massacres become vital'. Wars are no longer in defence of a sovereign, but of a people, its health and – as I want to argue is increasingly the case – its 'way of life'or culture. But that is to get ahead of ourselves, for Foucault in the *History of Sexuality*, as for Mujkic, what is at stake, is 'the biological existence of a population':

if genocide is indeed the dream of modern powers, this is not because of a recent return of the ancient right to kill; it is because power is situated and exercised at the level of life, the species, the race, and the large scale phenomena of population.

(1980: 137)

The paradigm case here is Nazi Germany. As Foucault noted in his 1975–76 lectures at the College de France: the biopolitical rationality that links power of life and power of death is race science. Killing is justified not primarily in terms of victory over adversaries, 'but in the elimination of the biological threat to and the improvement of the species or race . . . Once the state functions in the biopower mode, racism alone can justify the murderous function of the state' (2003: 256).

Foucault himself resisted those in the audience who suggested a continuity between the 'blood and honour' discourse of the medieval race wars and modern race science. Valverde concurs. But she thinks that Foucault may have overstated the role of scientific and medical knowledge in his account of modern racism and massacres. 'Race science was very important for the Nazis, but later "ethnic cleansings" have often reverted to the old "race wars" discourse about lost national honour, instead of using modern science' (2007: 176–77). Citing the example of Bosnian–Serbian struggles and the theology of American neo-conservatives, she suggests:

> Perhaps 'biopolitics' can be stretched to include anti-scientific knowledges, whether of religion or of how to look after one's health. And perhaps biopolitics could be said also to include the currently popular culturalist politics of 'the clash of civilizations'; the cultural essentialism that is current today is not very different, in form, from the sort of essentialism that was better known to Foucault, that which relies on anthropological and biomedical knowledges of human difference.

(Valverde 2007: 177)

Scientific sectarianism, cultural pluralism and the development of the peace process in Northern Ireland

Tracing the development of normative ethnicity in Northern Ireland we have noted two governmental mechanisms that rely on compulsory group identification: designation rules in the legislature and fair employment legislation. The latter preceded the former, and both should be seen in the context of debate surrounding the 1991 census.

Biopolitical calculations are inbuilt to Northern Ireland as it was created in 1921 as the largest area in which a majority for the union with Britain could be sustained. Fear of Catholic fecundity influenced the response of the union-ist government to social and welfare legislation that was introduced in Britain after the Second World War, and which would normally have been introduced to Northern Ireland as a matter of course. Elections have long been charac-terised as a 'sectarian headcount'. However, in the period leading up to the IRA ceasefire in 1994 and the signing of the GFA in 1998 speculation as to the population balance between the two communities was raised to a higher level – in terms of pitch and sophistication – than ever before.

This time the headcount was prompted by the publication of results from the 1991 census, the first since 1971 thought to be reasonably accurate.[1] Two items excited political and media interest. First, 'comparisons with 1971 seemed to confirm a growing sectarian "apartheid" which many had long suspected'. Second, 'the statistics apparently heralded a decisive shift in the sectarian balance of power in favour of Catholic nationalists, both in Northern Ireland as a whole and in particular areas' (Anderson and Shuttleworth 1994: 74). The statistics linked well with a broader discourse then current regarding the retreat, if not quite yet, defeat of Unionism (see Finlay 2001a).

One of the key protagonists in the debate about the significance of the 1991 census was Tim Pat Coogan, a Dublin-based newspaper-man and historian.

> In the case of the demographic argument, I began using it when the IRA cease-fires hung in the balance, so as to persuade the waverers that there was no point in continuing warfare for something which was coming shortly anyhow. Later, when the peace process was established, I tried to point out to the unionist community that if they did not cut a deal now they would be swept away in the not too distant future.
>
> (*Ireland on Sunday* 19 September 1999)

Whatever about Coogan's retrospective justification for his rhetoric, it would appear that the 'demographic argument' had some effect. In the period after the signing of the GFA, *The Irish Times* reported

> Widespread briefing of provisional IRA members . . . that the armed struggle is over . . . there would be no further point in continuing vio-lence, as within '10 to 15 years' there would be sufficient 'demographic' change in the North's population to provide for a nationalist majority in favour of reintegration.
>
> (25 April 1998; also see Friel 2002)

Group survival and reproduction was thus an issue of political calculation during the Irish peace process. Mujkic's assertion that ethnopolitics equals biopolitics would appear to apply here as well as in the much fiercer conditions of Bosnia-Herzegovina. The equation of ethnopolitics and biopolitics has implications as to the kind of knowledge that is brought to bear on the topic of population balance, reproduction and group security. Foucault would lead us to look for expert knowledges, and sure enough, in the debates that preceded the ceasefires and the Agreement, we see the emergence of what Anderson and Shuttleworth call 'scientific sectarianism'. As they point out in their analysis of the 1991 debate, 'the focus on census data and statistical analysis' and 'crude empiricism' gave the debate 'objectivity' (1994: 80). Moreover the various protagonists drew on a range of experts, statisticians and demographers, albeit often quoted anonymously (Gudgin 2002).

Of particular significance in the development of scientific sectarianism and normative ethnicity is a meeting of the Statistical and Social Inquiry Society of Ireland, Ireland's oldest social science organisation,[2] in May 1994. At the meeting Edgar Jardine, an employee of the research division of the Northern Ireland civil service read a paper entitled 'Demographic Structure in Northern Ireland and its Implications for Constitutional Preference'. Among the discussants were Professor Brendan Walsh, an expert from the Economic and Social Research Institute, the main social research institute in the Republic of Ireland, and former Taoiseach, Garret FitzGerald.

Jardine, Walsh and FitzGerald all agree that the assessment of the demographic and constitutional implications of the 1991 census turns on two sets of assumptions. First, about the relationship between declared religion/community background and supposed constitutional preference (i.e. for the status quo or for a united Ireland). Second, assumptions about those respondents who either declared that they had no religion (3.7 per cent) or who failed to state a religious denomination (7.3 per cent) – 11 per cent in all (Jardine 1994: 196). What is remarkable is that while all three experts seem willing to question assumptions about the relationship between religion/community and constitutional preference, they seem determined on the idea that everyone in Northern Ireland has a stable religious/communal identity and that the 11 per cent could and should be reallocated to their 'true' religion/community. They differed only as to which was the true religion/community: Jardine and FitzGerald thought the balance of the 11 per cent should be allocated to the protestant group, Walsh to the Roman Catholic group.

Alone among the three, Walsh entertains the idea that 'There is a case for not analyzing the "*Not Stated* and *No Religion* population" any further, on the grounds that this is the preferred status of the respondents, who do not wish to be recorded as belonging to any religious group'. But he immediately rejects the idea:

> there is a sense in which in Northern Ireland a person *must be* from either a Catholic or protestant community, and the religious question is of most interest as a clue to the distribution of the population between these communities.
>
> (1994: 211, my emphasis)

As we shall see in the next chapter, Garret FitzGerald did some of the intellectual and practical ground work for the peace process when he was Taoiseach between 1981 and 1987. Writing in 1997, he referred back to the debate at the Statistical and Social Inquiry Society of Ireland to justify an assertion that the words 'Catholic' and 'protestant' no longer refer to religious denomination, but to 'cultural background': 'those who identi-fied themselves as having no religion or who did not state a religion in the 1991 census are classified as culturally Catholic or protestant' (FitzGerald 1997). According to FitzGerald and the other experts who participated in the debate at the Statistical and Social Inquiry Society of Ireland everyone in Northern Ireland must be a member of one or other community. In line with this logic the most recent census held in 2001 confronted those not indicating 'a current religious identity' with a supplementary question 'to indicate the religious community they had been brought up in' (Osborne 19 December 2002). Communal identity appears ineluctable so far as the state and its agencies are concerned.

Consociational theorists do not participate in this debate. But it is worth noting that as part of a speculative discussion about 'engineering' conditions in Northern Ireland so as to be more favourable to consociation, McGarry and O'Leary mention Catholic population growth so as to improve the balance of power (1995: 325). Given their nervousness around the notion of culture noted in the previous chapter, it is interesting that here they have no hesita-tion in endorsing FitzGerald's notion of 'cultural Catholics' and 'cultural protestants'(McGarry and O'Leary 1995: 502).

Cultural pluralism, equality legislation and telling the difference

The term 'scientific sectarianism' is eye-catching, but misleading. It sounds too much like old-style 'scientific racism', based in spurious biological and physical differences. What Anderson and Shuttleworth call scientific sec-tarianism is more like contemporary racism, which is rooted in notions of cultural difference and pluralism (see Valverde 2007 and Hardt and Negri 2000). Cultural markers of difference are no more valid than physical markers of difference. But this hasn't prevented the administrators of difference from trying itemise them.

In Northern Ireland the official, indeed legal, effort to elaborate markers of difference congruent with cultural pluralism takes place around the same time or just before the man from the research division of the Northern Ireland civil service would have begun thinking about his paper to the Statistical and Social Inquiry Society of Ireland. The context was not the census, but the fair employment legislation mentioned in Chapter 2. Allow me to provide some background.

Discrimination against Catholics in housing and employment was a key issue in civil rights protests that preceded the onset of the Troubles. In 1976 a Fair Employment Agency was established to combat religious discrimination. By the mid-1980s it was becoming apparent that the 1976 legislation was not having the desired effect: Catholic men were still two and half times more likely to be unemployed than protestant men. Following a campaign led by the Irish (American) National Caucus that sought to make United States investment in Northern Ireland firms conditional on their acceptance of affirmative action in the employment of Catholics (the 'MacBride Principles'), the British Government introduced proposals to strengthen fair employment legislation and to create a new Fair Employment Commission.

The legislation introduced to the British parliament in 1989 made provision for the monitoring of the religious composition of workforces and job applicants, but left it open to employees and job applicants to designate their own identities. The Shadow Secretary of State objected to this arrangement, and urged that the main methods of monitoring be specified. Christopher McCrudden (2007: 319), a leading advocate of consociation and member of SACHR 1984–88, who also advised the Shadow Secretary of State, observed:

> Concern was expressed . . . [that] relying only on answers provided by individuals as to their community affiliation would be liable to result in inaccurate figures. There was a fear that there would be systematic and organized resistance to providing information on community affiliation as part of a sustained campaign of resistance against the legislation, and that this would lead to the other provisions of the regulatory scheme that relied on accurate figures becoming a dead letter. As a result of these arguments the government agreed to introduce amendments . . .

to ensure that several methods should be available to employers, not just the method of asking direct question of the employee.

(2007: 329–30)

Under legislation first introduced in 1989, monitoring was conducted as follows. Employers were required to ask employees and job applicants about their communal identity. The employee or job applicant was given three options: s/he can be 'a member of the protestant community; a member of the Roman Catholic community; or a member of neither the protestant nor the Roman Catholic in Northern Ireland'. According to advice given by the Fair Employment Commission the third 'grouping will mainly apply to people who were born *outside* Northern Ireland' (ATGWU 1993: 9, my emphasis). In cases where a direct question – the 'principal method' – does not elicit the communal category to which the employee or job applicant belongs, the employer is 'strongly recommended' to apply a 'residuary method' (McCrudden 2007: 330). The residuary method allows the employer to draw on other relevant information provided in writing by the employee or job applicant to allocate them to a communal category:

> the following qualifies as relevant information: surname and other names; address; schools attended by the employee . . . the employee's sporting or other leisure pursuits; clubs, societies or other organizations to which he or she belongs; or the occupation as clergyman or minister of a particular religious denomination or as teacher in a particular school, of any referee nominated by the employee when he or she applied for the job.
>
> (McCrudden 2007: 330–31)

McCrudden describes the 'residuary method' as a 'reasonable method . . . of establishing identity that facilitates the implementation of the legislation' (McCrudden 2007: 330–31). He describes the criteria used as part of the 'residuary method' to allocate people to a communal category against their will as being 'generally reliable ways of "telling" religio-political origin in Northern Ireland'.

The use of the word 'telling' and the quotes that wrap it are interesting here, for it alludes to a phenomenon that was first described by Rosemary Harris. According to her analysis, the religious or ethnic dichotomy is so pervasive in Northern Ireland that in everyday life it is crucial 'to be able to determine the allegiances of strangers'. So much so 'that many Ulster people seem to have developed an extreme sensitivity to signs . . . that denote the affiliations of those that they meet'. McCrudden does not cite Harris or any subsequent study of 'telling'(see Finlay 1999 and 2001b for a summary of this literature) perhaps because analysts of 'telling' keep a skeptical distance as to the validity of the criteria used to 'tell' and note some of the nefarious uses to which they are put.

Harris describes the use of 'telling' in everyday face-to-face interaction to manage the alienation of a deeply plural society; for example, the avoidance of causing offence or embarrassment by saying the wrong thing to the wrong person. The result is that even close neighbours can remain strangers locked in mutual incomprehension. Frank Burton notes that the same criteria are used 'when the identity of an individual is being determined for intended military, political and criminal activity' (1978: 65).[3] Feldman (1991) has described 'telling' as the embodiment of sectarianism, for at the level of everyday, face-to-face interaction, the criteria used to 'tell' include not just name, school attended, residence and so forth but also, according to adepts, aspects of one's 'physical appearance, expression and manner, style of dress and speech idiom to provide the clues that will enable the correct categorisation to be made' (Harris 1986: 148).

The use of 'telling' to allocate individuals to a communal category against their will, and the extraordinary apparatus developed to enable administrators to effect such categorisation is justified on the basis of a fear that without it, fair employment provisions would be subverted by people designating a false communal identity. It is worth pausing briefly to consider this fear, for here I can draw on my experience as an evaluator of a programme that aimed to inform trade union officials and activists about the new fair employment legislation.[4] The programme was organised by a large trade union, and funded by the Northern Ireland Office through the Central Community Relations Unit. The programme involved conferences and workshops attended by trade union officials and shop stewards.

McCrudden's fear is not unreasonable as unionist parties were hostile to the introduction of the legislation, but it may be exaggerated (see Hadden 2008). It is true that unionist scaremongering created the belief that the legislation would allow for reverse discrimination. I recall one participant in a workshop explaining that some protestant workers feared that they were going to be put out of work in order to create work for that Catholic community. Overall, though, the mood amongst shop stewards was resignation rather than rebellion.

Looking back, the only objection to compulsory categorisation that I can recall was the potentially adverse effect of making such a declaration on workplace relations. I cannot recall anyone objecting in principle. With this in mind it is worth pointing out that the new legislation on religious discrimination was contextualised in terms of discrimination on other grounds, notably gender, and sold to trade union activists in terms of a *universalistic* ideal of fairness. Moreover, I don't think it occurred to anyone involved in the programme at the time, certainly not to myself, that compulsory communal categorisation would become a central plank of the post-conflict constitution.

This last observation is a further corrective to any temptation to teleology. The legal scholar who advised government on the design of legislation for monitoring employment was to become a prominent advocate of consociation. He retrospectively uses this legislation to defend the denial of a right of exit or a right to self-identification in the proposed Bill of Rights for Northern Ireland. The justification of the employment legislation and of the denial of a right of exit are both rooted in the scholarly literature on Northern Ireland as a plural society; nevertheless, it would be foolish to suggest a seamless, linear development from one to the other.

Conclusion

Even though the degree of blood-letting and ethnic-cleansing in Northern Ireland was on a much, much lesser scale than in Bosnia, we can see that a rhetoric of ethnic reproduction and survival of the group figured very strongly as an issue in the development of the peace process. Alongside everyday sectarian or ethnic politics and intertwined with them we have traced the development of official practices and techniques in the census and in employment monitoring that make ethnicity normative. Asim Mujkic's application of the notion of biopolitics to ethnopolitics has proved useful in drawing our attention to these phenomena. It has also drawn our attention to the role of various experts in this: a social researcher employed in the civil service, a learned society, an academic lawyer invoking the work of a social anthropologist who pioneered pluralist perspectives in Ireland.

But at this point we need to proceed cautiously. Caution is required because, as flagged at the outset of this chapter, Foucault emphasised the extent to which biopolitics were based in scientific and medical expertise. 'Our' experts come mainly from the human and social sciences, but it is reassuring for our argument to note the salience of statisticians and demographers.

We also need to be mindful of another issue. Rabinow and Rose point out the defining feature of biopolitics is not only that it depends on scientific knowledge but that it is concerned with 'the "vital" character of living human beings'. Biopolitics are concerned with the good of the population and the individuals who constitute it, and it is from this concern that biopolitics draws

its normative power 'to qualify, measure, appraise, and heirarchize' to 'effect
. . . distributions around the norm' (Foucault 1980: 144). We saw in Chapter
3 that discourses regarding 'cultural identity are centrally concerned with
the vital character of human existence'. This is worth exploring more fully
through institutions and practices that operationalise this idea.

5   Consociationalism as a form of liberal governmentality

'Single-identity work' versus community relations

Foucault's discussion of biopower/biopolitics in the *History of Sexuality* is part of a larger genealogy of power that culminates in the discussion of governmentality in his posthumously published lectures at the College de France. Here is how Rabinow and Rose explain the relationship between the terms biopolitics and governmentality in the overall development of Foucault's thinking:

> Whilst initially linking biopolitics to the regulatory endeavors of developing states he recognizes that 'the great overall regulations that proliferated throughout the nineteenth century are also found at the sub-state level, in a whole series of sub-state institutes such as medical institutions, welfare funds, insurance, and so on' . . . This is the point at which Foucault begins to develop his concept of 'governmentality' to encompass the variety of ways of problematizing and acting on individual and collective conduct in the name of certain objectives which do not have the State as their origin or point of reference. And as he develops this line of thought, he distances himself from the view that such power over life is unambiguously nefarious.
>
> (2003:7)

It's not just the concept of governmentality that is useful, but also the implicit methodology. Marianna Valverde draws an illuminating contrast between Foucault and contemporaneous theorists of the state like Louis Althusser and Nicos Poulantzas and latter day Focauldians who sketch large abstract schemes of epochal change. While Althusser and Poulantzas were stacking abstraction upon abstraction, Foucault 'preferred historical inquiries into "minor" practices for governing people and spaces used by state as well as by non-state institutions' (Valverde 2007: 160). Valverde describes Foucault's focus on the practices of government – not 'the epochs or generalized modes of power-knowledge' – as a 'methodological revolution', which brings Foucault into constellation with sociologists such as Erving Goffman who 'demonstrated that social power relations do not leap from structural economic relations, but are instead made and re-made every day in the encounters among individuals and groups that make up institutions' (2007: 160). In this chapter I will re-examine the development of the peace process using a Foucauldian approach to power and government or what he called 'governmentality'.

The word 'governmentality' is a play on the words 'government' and 'rationality'. It draws our attention to the political rationalities – the variable forms of truth, knowledge and expertise – that make reality legible and therefore amenable to government. One of the characteristics of these political rationalities is that they are problem orientated. Governmental intervention is justified through the definition of events or groups or social things as being problematic, with causes that can be understood.

These political rationalities consist in discursive means of rendering reality intelligible but the point is that in doing so they make it amenable to intervention through the design of programs, techniques and practices that seek to influence the conduct of individuals or groups and resolve problems. How do these programmes/techniques/practices seek to influence conduct? Not primarily through coercion. That form of power, says Foucault, belongs more to pre-modern sovereign power of the police state. Coercion remains an option, but as Inda points out modern governmental practices and programs seek to influence conduct by 'cultivating particular types of individual and collective identity as well as forms of agency and subjectivity'(2005: 10). Studies of governmentality have drawn our attention to a wide variety of such practices and programmes. Notable amongst these are, 'standardized tactics for the training and implantation of habits; pedagogic, therapeutic and punitive techniques of reformation and cure' (2005: 9). Foucault himself was particularly concerned to show how programmes and institutions that ostensibly and self-professedly had nothing to do with political power – universities for instance – were deeply implicated in the project of regulation and discipline.

The notion of conflict resolution is a case in point. As Jenny Edkins says: 'the idea that conflicts have causes, and that if we could understand what those causes were we could remove them and put an end to conflict, reflects a specifically modernist, Western . . . approach, where answers are sought in technical terms' (2006: 503).

Consociationalism is more than a form of conflict resolution. It is a mode of liberal governmentality that is *informed by* and cultivates particular forms of ethno-national subjectivity. We have discussed in broad terms the theories of plural society, culture, ethnicity, nationalism and identity that provide the political rationality that underpins and authorises this form of governmentality. But this discussion has been conducted at a fairly abstract level. Here, in the spirit of Foucault's approach to government and the state, I want to look at the institutional practices of consociational government. This chapter is concerned with approaches to conflict resolution developed in the period leading to the GFA and thereafter with a focus on cultural and community relations programmes.

Consociational governmentality and the subversion of community relations work

Counter to the precepts of consociation which stress the virtue of cultural autonomy and communal segregation with dialogue taking place only at the elite level, the traditional approach to community relations and conflict resolution in Northern Ireland as elsewhere stresses the importance of dialogue between members of conflicted groups. This is based on the twin ideas, usually attributed to the psychologist Gordon Allport (1954), that, first, conflict is a product of prejudice and, second, prejudice is a product of ignorance or lack of shared experience. If these assumptions are true, dialogue is the answer. This kind of approach underpinned the efforts of the first community relations programme devised in response to the onset of the troubles in 1969.[1]

How then was community relations practice brought more into line with consociational rationality? Again the role of the Standing Advisory Commission on Human Rights (SACHR) is central. To remind the reader, SACHR coined the key phrase 'parity of esteem' which provides the rationale for the cultural autonomy of two communities in Northern Ireland. SACHR's warrant was the Anglo-Irish Agreement of 1987 which obliged the British Government to introduce 'measures to recognise and accommodate the rights and identities of the two traditions in Northern Ireland' (1990: 84). To this end the British government 'established a Community Relations Council whose functions include the fostering of both traditions within Northern Ireland' (1990: 89).

In fact, even before the signing of the Anglo-Irish Agreement, SACHR had already commissioned a review of community relations. *Improving Community Relations* by Hugh Frazer and Mari Fitzduff was first published in 1986 and was re-issued in several editions. The third edition, published by the Community Relations Council in 1994, was available online until very recently. The key outcome of the review was the need for a new community relations agency to act as a focal point for community organisations and a set of recommendations as to how it should proceed.

Frazer and Fitzduff, echo Allport's contact hypothesis:

> Prejudice is often based on assumptions about the other 'group' which are not necessarily our subjective experience, but untested or *inherited* assumptions. Much reconciliation work – particularly that which focuses on experiences of a primarily 'contact' kind, is based on the idea that if one group actually gets to know the other, then the reality of the other grouping's favourable aspects will be revealed and mutual respect will develop.
>
> (Frazer and FitzDuff 1994: 11, my emphasis)

And they recommend that contact initiatives remain a part of the new agency's brief. But they also note obstacles to the success of programmes promoting contact and dialogue: 'For those who hold convictions so strongly that they leave no room for compromise with others whose convictions differ, such programmes may prove useless, and different programmes must be developed' (1994: 12). Like the other experts we've discussed, Frazer and FitzDuff allude to the rich stream of work on 'telling' starting with Rosemary Harris and Frank Burton which shows that 'Contact can take place among people without much real communication' (1994: 20; see also Finlay 1999). And they urge a realistic assessment of what 'projects using contact tactics as their method' are likely to achieve: 'while contact with members of other groups rarely proves deleterious to relationships, it is unlikely to prove sufficient to change hostile attitudes unless accompanied by both active discussion programmes and possibilities for long term involvement and contact' (1994: 23).

With hindsight one can begin to detect here the beginnings of a move towards programmes and practices that are more consistent with the consociational emphasis on cultural autonomy. Thus, there is a 'need to investigate the function of cultural identity in group and intergroup relations' (1994: 25), and they recommend that a new community relations agency should:

> encourage Cultural Awareness and Mutual Understanding Projects which will help groups to explore *their own* culture and heritage with the aim of developing a new awareness and appreciation of their own and other traditions and a recognition of the developing nature of identity and culture.
>
> (1994: 30, my emphasis)

When the new central community relation agency was established it supported the formation in 1988 of the Cultural Traditions Group whose initial aim was to encourage each community to explore their own culture and heritage. As we shall see, the Cultural Traditions Group's work always involved mutual understanding as well as self-understanding, and indeed it eventually renamed itself as the Cultural Diversity Group, but it pioneered an approach which was to become more and more prevalent – namely 'single-identity work'.

Cheyanne Church *et al.* (2004: 289) present the development of single-identity work as being a product of 'frustration and practicality, more so than theoretical principles'.

The cross-community approach to conflict resolution has failed:

> despite the multitude of cross-community initiatives aimed at overcoming communal divisions during the past thirty years – among them such projects as reconciliation groups, residential centers, publicity projects, cultural traditions work, institutional anti-sectarian work, training, and cross-border initiative – viable reconciliation has not been achieved in this society.
>
> (2004: 281)

The reasons given by Church *et al.* for this failure are more or less the same as those adduced by Frazer and Fitzduff: ethnic segregation is profound and difficult to overcome and there are those whose convictions are so deep that they refuse to meet with the other side. Single-identity work, they say, emerged to deal with such people who refused to engage in cross-community contact, and was conducted in the hope that it might lead to a more traditional community relation situation.

However, Church *et al.* (2004) also allude to the growth of single-identity work of a different kind: that is, work that is conceived as an end in itself. They note that this kind of work has two kinds of purpose or rationale: 'own culture validation' and 'personal development projects where the chief focus is on building the *self-esteem* of group members' (Church *et al.* 2004: 284, my emphasis). These purposes seem consistent with the rationale of 'parity of esteem' and cultural autonomy, which would belie Church *et al.*'s suggestion that single-identity work is untheorised. Church *et al.* plausibly associate the traditional approach to cross-community work with Gordon Allport's contact hypothesis, but they fail to recognise that the theoretical rationale underpinning single-identity work is provided by the notions of culture and identity that I have traced to the culture and personality school of anthropology and Erik Erikson – ideas that rivalled Allport in post-war

America, and indeed were partly elaborated in opposition to Allport's ideas (Gleason 1983).

In other words, the old anthropological idea of culture might usefully be thought of as the 'truth discourse' that licenses single-identity work. What I have in mind is Rabinow and Rose's definition of biopower as involving

> one or more truth discourses about the 'vital' character of living human beings; an array of authorities considered competent to speak that truth; strategies for intervention upon collective existence in the name of life and health; and modes of subjectification, in which individuals work on themselves in the name of individual or collective life or health.
>
> (2003: 10)

The key truth of the old idea of culture is that being rooted or grounded in a strong communal culture is vital to one's character, integrity and sense of self; in other words that personal identity is dependent on communal identity. Single identity work is counter-intuitive and cuts against traditional approaches to community relations, rooted in the Allport's contact hypothesis. It has evolved as a practical response to real difficulties. Community relations experts worry about it,[2] and as we shall see in Chapter 9, those worries have intensified. All this is true, but it is not accurate to describe single-identity work as untheorised, and seen in the light of the ideas about culture and identity developed by Erikson, it makes perfect sense. Who were the 'array of authorities' who spoke this awkward truth locally?

The authorities who spoke the truth about culture, community, identity

Foremost among the few intellectual debts Frazer and Fitzduff acknowledge are the Commission for Racial Equality in Britain, and other British organisations seeking 'solutions . . . to the problem of racial disharmony' (1994: 9). This is in line with most commentators on community relations who stress the role of the British state (see McVeigh and Rolston 2007), though Rolston's (1980) analysis of the first Community Relations Commission, established in 1969, discusses wider influences; for example, the influence of counterinsurgency work in British Colonies (1980: 152–53) and of policy responses to ethnic and racial conflict in the United States.[3]

Responding to this kind of analysis (2002) Bryan has argued that community relations are not a policy idea invented by the British state; they are part of a process, within which some, including representatives of the state, certainly have more power than others, but a process which is negotiated by a range of interests . . . to simply assume that the state is pathological . . . whatever that means, that its interests are unified, and to ignore the complexity of negotiation between the state and groups of people is to ignore a much more difficult analysis of social process.

(Bryan 2006: 610)

I would agree with Bryan when he argues that community relations are not a policy idea invented by the British state: in the literature on community relations policy and the peace process and process more generally, too much emphasis has been placed on the overweening agency of the British state. I also agree with Bryan that community relations policy involved negotiation with a range of interests: the literature has paid a lot of attention to the role of local parties and 'civil society'. But so much attention has been paid to local agents and to the British State, that the main sources of intellectual authority have been missed. If you want to find the array of authorities who spoke the awkward truth about the importance of 'own culture validation', parity of esteem and so forth, one has to look to the Irish intellectuals and the Irish State.

In Chapter 3 we traced the ultimate legislative sanction for these ideas to the Anglo-Irish Agreement. In the wake of this agreement, the British government did indeed introduce 'measures to recognise and accommodate the rights and identities of the two traditions in Northern Ireland'(SACHR 1990: 84). Notable amongst these measures was the formation of a new Community Relations Council and within that overarching structure, the Cultural Traditions Groups (CTG)[4], which pioneered single-identity work.

It is widely acknowledged that the Anglo-Irish Agreement gave the Irish state a say in the governance of Northern Ireland, and there is some appreciation of the agreement as a triumph of Irish diplomacy, but given the emphasis on the role of the British state in the literature on on community relation policy, there is little appreciation of the role played by revisionist Irish intellectuals in framing the Anglo-Irish Agreement and the provisions it makes for community relations. In the specifically Irish context, revisionism refers to a movement of historians and politicians spanning several generations which sought to replace the monocultural vision of Irish identity projected in traditional nationalist historiography with a more pluralist vision. It was this revisionist movement that provided the array of authorities who spoke the awkward truth about the importance of cultural identity. Indeed the Irish

Taoiseach who signed the Anglo-Irish Agreement, Garret FitzGerald, was a leading revisionist in the 1970s.

Truth discourses, political rationalities – whatever you want to call them – work by making reality legible and therefore amenable to government, and they do this by identifying problems to be solved. For revisionists the underlying problem in Ireland was a clash of cultural identities. Thus F. S. L. Lyons (1979) argued that there was not one singular Irish identity, but two or three or more discrete cultural identities. In developing his argument, he strains to define culture in a broader way than was conventional in Irish historiography at the time. He starts with Matthew Arnold's definition of culture as that which 'makes the best that has been thought and known in the world current everywhere', and which serves 'to make all men live in an atmosphere of sweetness and light'. Lyons comments,

> When Arnold was composing his essay in the late 1860s, the social sciences were still in their infancy. There were no *social anthropologists or social psychologists* to compel him to explain himself more intelligibly . . . To get closer to Irish realities we shall have to interpret culture in a much broader sense, yet without committing ourselves irrevocably to the devotees of any specific school . . . At this stage . . . it will be enough to apply it to the different groups in Ireland which either have or have had a distinct and relatively autonomous existence and whose members have shared a recognizably *common way of life.*
>
> (1979: 3, my emphasis)

Thus, although Lyons refuses to commit himself to any 'specific school' of anthropology, he invokes what we have called the old idea of culture. Using this idea, Lyons develops a famously bleak analysis in which Ireland's political troubles are merely the outward sign of the never-ending clash of underlying cultural differences and aspirations.

This is the pluralist political rationality that underpins the GFA and, I would argue, consociationalism more generally. In the previous chapters I have highlighted the influence of early theorists of pluralism, like Rosemary Harris and M. G. Smith (1971) on Lijphart, but I do not want to give the impression of seamless progression. Dean describes the genealogical approach to intellectual history as

> a way of linking historical contents into organised and ordered trajectories that are neither a simple unfolding of their origins or the necessary realisation of their ends. It is a way of analysing multiple, open-ended,

heterogeneous trajectories of discourses, practices, and events, and of establishing their patterned relationship, without recourse to regimes of truth that claim pseudo-naturalistic laws or global necessities.

(Dean 1994: 35–36)

What needs to be emphasised here is that at the time when it came to fruition in the early 1980s, the revisionist approach to the Northern Ireland 'problem' appeared quite new and innovative. For example, Garret FitzGerald added an additional twist to the pluralist analysis. In addition to the clash of cultures, there was also a specifically Eriksonian problem; namely an identity crisis. Worse, it was 'a double identity crisis' (1976: 139) one afflicting nationalists and the other unionists, both an outcome of 'the traumatic psychological impact upon the island' of partition. I will return to FitzGerald's analysis in the next chapter, but for the moment I want to stick with Lyons for he was the presiding spirit at the founding conference of the Cultural Traditions Group.

The keynote speaker at the founding conference of the group was Roy Foster (1989), the leading member of the new generation of revisionist historians. Foster starts with Lyons (1979) and agrees that the source of Ireland's political problems are conflicts and confusions of cultural identity, but what was required of Foster was that he render Lyons's pessimism as optimism: Foster has to show that culture could yet redeem. If the reader recalls, before settling on the old idea of culture, Lyon's had discussed Matthew Arnold's view of culture as that which 'makes the best that has been thought and known in the world current everywhere', and which serves 'to make all men live in an atmosphere of sweetness and light'. Amongst some of the discussants at the conference, this Arnoldian project is amalgamated with a view of Northern Ireland or Ulster as a distinct region with its own culture and personality, shared by people from both communities. Foster cites Rosemary Harris' ethnography in support of this notion of a shared regional culture.

The conflation of different concepts of culture enables the conference participants to imagine that if Catholics and protestants were encouraged to look into their own traditions and communal identities they would gain in self-respect and self-esteem such that they would have the confidence to engage with the other community and to learn about its traditions. In the process there would develop not only mutual respect, each community would discover that they shared values rooted in a common regional culture. Some projects followed this pattern, but, as Church *et al.* (2004) note, many stopped at the first stage, giving birth to what has become known as single-identity work.

Consociationalists themselves did not play a big part in these debates. McGarry and O'Leary (1995) were suspicious of cultural traditions work, but in line with the ideas of their mentor (see Lijphart 1975: 104) they reject Allport's contact hypothesis (2009: 374) and 'mixing and fixing' approaches to community relations and education more generally (2004: 187). Again they cite Rosemary Harris in support of their position. Like her, they think that cultural differences between Catholics and protestants in Northern Ireland are slight. Following Michael Ignatieff (1993) they invoke Freud's notion of the narcissism of minor differences, and end up with something close to FitzGerald's notion that the conflict is caused by crises of identity:

> the smaller the real differences between two peoples the larger they are bound to loom in their imagination. We would prefer to express this insight in the following way: the more cultural differences there are, and the deeper they are, then the greater the likelihood that collective identities will be secure rather than threatened.
>
> (1995: 253)

Consociationalists may not have played a large part in debates about approaches to community relations, but consociational theory is consistent with the logic of single-identity work and of 'own culture validation', which is to make identities more secure.

Conclusion

The argument developing through this chapter has been that if a theory of 'plural society' provides the political rationale for a consociational form of liberal governmentality, the problem that authorises this form of governmentality is a view of political conflict as being the product of an underlying clash and confusion of ethnic or ethno-national identity. Amongst the various programmes implemented before and after the GFA, those aimed at improving community relations based on Allport's contact hypothesis are not the key ones, but rather separatist pedagogic projects for children and adults that are aimed at resolving crises and confusions of identity and promoting authenticity and self-esteem.

In Northern Ireland these projects are known as 'single-identity' work. And yet there seems to be a lack of conviction or uncertainty about them: the idea that dialogue and mutual understanding might be the way forward persists as does the idea that culture might yet redeem. Thus the same confused logic espoused by the Cultural Traditions Group – culture as the source of division and of redemption – is reproduced by international consultants advising on cultural policy in Bosnia-Herzegovina. According to the rationale of a programme created by the Council of Europe for the evaluation of European cultural policies:

> In no country in Europe is cultural policy more important than in Bosnia and Herzegovina. Culture is both the cause and the solution to its problems. 'It is the cause,' explains Landry, 'because cultural arguments were used to divide the country and to turn the different groups against each other in an orgy of destruction; it is the solution because culture might be able to bring people back together again through initiating cultural programmes and activity that increase mutual understanding.'
>
> (Kalender 2008; Landry 2002:13)

Amongst community relations practitioners themselves, one can find in Bosnia-Herzegovina the same practical wisdom as in Northern Ireland regarding the limitations of cross community or 'trans-ethnic' work: 'we had 50 years of common curricula, overall social and political promotion of brotherhood and unity . . . and it did not prevent us to shoot each other'.[5] And there is a similar appreciation of the usefulness of working with a 'single community' group as a way of 'opening the community for inter-ethnic communication'. For example, Kosovan Nansen Dialogue, a non-governmental agency, works with Kosovan Serbs who are distrustful of the Kosovo Albanians and consequently lack 'willingness to engage in any kind of communication with the Albanian community'. The aim of this program is to improve the 'motivation of the Kosovan Serb community to take part in interethnic dialogue' (2007). The idea of single-identity work as an end in itself seems remote. Community relations work in Bosnia-Herzegovina tends to be funded mostly by international donors rather than the state, and international donors remain leery of single-identity work.[6]

In the formal education sector, the logic seems to be towards cultural validation. Ugo Vlaisavljevic and Asim Mujkic speak of the role of the universities in the 'reappropriation of cultural heritage' (Vlaisavljevic 1998) and 'the production of national being . . . authenticity and pureness':

> This task of reappropriation is entrusted to the humanities faculty, the departments of History, Literature, Philosophy, National Language, and the like, but also to certain of the social sciences, such as Political Science. Professors of the humanities in Bosnia have put themselves

forward as formulators and interpreters of 'ethnic' narratives. They view themselves as undertaking a sort of archaeology, digging out the 'authentic' elements of a community or collective. Their 'findings' and narratives are mainly of a mythical and religious nature. These narratives serve to promote the construction of ethnic ideologies. Various academic disciplines take it as their task to explain the content of a certain kinship or collective identity, thus giving scientific legitimacy to ethnopolitics.

(Mujkic 2007: 122)

Primary and secondary education in Bosnia-Herzegovina are subject to an ongoing process of segregation, sanctioned by the Dayton constitution (1995 Article II, paragraph 3 and 4). In Ireland education has always been segregated with a rational of articulating the 'ethos' of various religious denominations, but since the signing of the GFA, the role of culture and heritage in the rationale for segregation has been strengthened. For example recent curriculum objectives stress 'culture' and define it as 'the artefacts, ideas and learned behaviour which makes up peoples' ways of life. The term "cultural heritage" should be taken to mean those elements of culture which are inherited' (Department of Education for Northern Ireland 2009: 6). Here too the logic appears to be 'own culture validation' and authenticity.

Looking at community relations programmes and cultural policy, we can see that exponents of what we might call the 'old' critique of consociation who complain about the institutionalisation of ethnicity and a failure to deliver on reconciliation are guilty of the same error that Foucault famously diagnosed in those who complained about the failure of the prison system to rehabilitate offenders. As Lijphart himself said, the point of consociation is not to weaken segmental cleavages but to make society more plural; that is, to recognise the cleavages explicitly and to turn them into constructive elements of stable democracy. (Lijphart 1977: 42; see also Porobić 2005). Notwithstanding the protestations of liberal consociationalists, the point of the community relations programmes and cultural policies in a consociational regime is not primarily reconciliation, but precisely the production of cultural autonomy and of exemplary ethno-national subjects.

6 Paradigm shifts and the production of 'national being'

When it returned in the late 1960s, the conflict in Ireland appeared as an anomaly in the western world. If that is no longer the case, it is partly to do with what subsequently happened in Yugoslavia and in parts of the former Soviet Union. But it's also a consequence of the successful normalisation of such conflicts: social science has made them legible and thence subject to rationalities and technologies of conflict management and government. The political rationality underpinning the techniques of conflict management is cultural pluralism. Equality is no longer seen as the main issue: conflicts are understood as being about belonging, aspiration and identity – sometimes long repressed.

In Chapters 2 and 3 I drew attention to the influence on Arend Lijphart, the pioneer of consociational approaches to governing conflict, of pluralist theory and sketched the role of anthropology in the development of cultural pluralism more generally. In Chapters 4 and 5 I outlined the practical application of pluralist ideas in the Irish case as part of the peace process, focussing on the development of programs aimed at community development and 'own culture validation'. Given the current hegemonic status of these ideas about culture and identity, what needs to be emphasised in this chapter is their novelty when they were introduced.[1]

Writing about interpretations of the Northern Ireland conflict, John Whyte uses the language of Thomas Kuhn. According to Whyte, the ideas about cultural pluralism upon which consociational governmentality draws were part of a Kuhnian paradigm shift that took place in the 1970s and 1980s. Whyte's language is fortuitous for it recalls Dreyfus and Rabinow's famous comparison of Kuhn's account of how sciences develop with Foucault's account of 'normalizing society' more generally:

> According to Kuhn a science becomes normal when the practitioners in a certain area all agree that a particular piece of work identifies the

important problems in a field and demonstrates how certain of these problems can be successfully solved. Kuhn calls such an agreed upon achievement a paradigm or exemplar . . . Paradigms set up normal science as the activity of finding certain puzzling phenomena which seem at first to resist incorporation into the theory, but which normal science . . . must ultimately account for in its own terms . . . normalizing technologies have an almost identical structure. They operate by establishing a common definition of goals and procedures, which take the form of manifestoes and, even more forcefully, agreed upon examples of how a well-ordered domain of human activity should be organized.

(1982: 197–98, my emphasis)

Juxtaposing the scientific and the programmatic – or knowledge and power – in this way is apt in the case of cultural pluralism. According to John Whyte, the idea that Ireland's problems are a product of underlying conflicts and confusions of identity emerged as rejection of traditional unionist, nationalist and Marxist views of the conflict. He further argues that the New Ireland Forum established in 1983 by Garret FitzGerald to bolster the constitutional nationalism of the Social, Democratic and Labour Party in the wake of hunger strikes by republican prisoners was the moment when the revisionist analysis began to supplant traditional thinking amongst the nationalists. The revisionist analysis of the conflict underpinned the subsequent diplomatic efforts that resulted in the Anglo-Irish Agreement. In the light of Dreyfus and Rabinow's juxtaposition of the scientific and the programmatic, revisionism provides a concrete example of how a new social science paradigm might acquire a strategic, programmatic, normative, normalising thrust.

The normalisation of the ethno-national

Political rationalities make reality legible and therefore amenable to government. Like scientific paradigms, political rationalities work by identifying problems. The problem that FitzGerald diagnosed was an Eriksonian one; that is, confusions and crises of identity. The problem with Northern Ireland was 'the failure of its inhabitants to develop any clear sense of identity' (1976: 137). He discerned 'a double identity crisis' (1976: 139): one afflicting Irish Republicans, one afflicting unionists, both an outcome of 'the traumatic psychological impact upon the island of a political division whose significance, and durability, were grossly underestimated by all at the time when it came into being' (1976: 139–40). Produced by the same event, partition, the two identity crises took different forms. For Irish Republicans it resided in the contradiction between a claim on all of the people of the island as Irish while simultaneously articulating an identity that was at heart Gaelic and Catholic (1976: 141). For unionists the identity crisis arose from a 'feeling of impermanence' a continuing 'sense of uncertainty and fear about their future': protestants never 'felt fully at home . . . in the land of their origins . . . or in that of their adoption'; that is, Britain and Ireland respectively (1976: 140). Though he doesn't say as much, FitzGerald's diagnosis of the protestant or unionist identity crisis alludes less to partition than to colonial origins. It was the classic predicament of a colonial settler community ill at ease with 'the land of their origins . . . or . . . of their adoption'. In any case, he clearly regarded the unionist identity crisis as being the more severe. Something that seemed to be confirmed by the violence of the unionist response to the Anglo-Irish Agreement FitzGerald signed with Margaret Thatcher in 1985. During the late 1980s and 1990s, the literature on the 'protestant identity crisis' and 'protestant alienation' grew large (see Finlay 2001). Part of the diagnosis of 'protestant identity crisis' was fragmentation (Gallagher 1995) and 'inarticulacy' – the inability of the leaders to express a position that was meaningful to powerful external agents and 'the international community'. From the perspective of governmentality, the problem is less 'protestant' inarticulacy than 'protestant illegibility'.

Perhaps the best exposition of this problem is Liam O'Dowd's comparison of unionist and Nationalist intellectuals (1991). O'Dowd's starting point is those authors who discuss the failure of northern protestants to develop a nationalism. The most well-known exponent of this view is Tom Nairn, but O'Dowd also mentions Terence Brown and David W. Miller both of whom regard 'the northern protestant' as being in,

> a kind of pre-nationalist condition, that he has seen his identity, if it can be called that, as being constructed in terms of a kind of Lockean contract, with regard to the relationship between the state and the individual. This means that an Ulster unionist, Ulster protestant, feels no need of that kind of confirmatory identity that the Irish nationalist project seem to imply as an absolute necessity for being fully human . . . He is loyal in a contractual relationship. When you belong to a nation, you have no choice in the matter: you are born into it, it is your spiritual destiny. The thing about a contract is that you are a party to it and, if the contract is broken, you can be released from the contract, and therefore concepts of identity, as understood by the nationalist, have little significance.
>
> (Brown 1992: 43)

Against this, O'Dowd argues:

> Lack of a *normal* national identity constructed by intellectuals should not be confused with a lack of an articulated . . . identity of an ethnic-religious nature . . . this identity was forged in historical interaction with, and in opposition to, the nationalist and Catholic movement in Ireland. As an 'imagined community'. . . its self image as a colony was important, as was its openness to the frequently racist ideology of British imperialism.
>
> (1991: 160–61, my emphasis)

Elsewhere, O'Dowd suggests that during 'the Troubles' the 'preoccupations of the . . . [colonial] settler' became sharper amongst loyalists, 'who in calmer times saw themselves as ethnic citizens (Ulster or Irish) of a multinational [United Kingdom] state' (1990: 39).

According to this analysis, the problem with protestants is that in the absence of 'a normal national identity constructed by intellectuals' they have remained wedded to forms of subjectivity based in an ostentatiously supremacist sectarian popular culture – a residue of colonialism promoted by institutions like the orange order. If this is the problem, the solution is to construct ethno-national rather than ethno-religious forms of subjectivity. As McGarry and O'Leary repeatedly say to critics who complain that the GFA institutionalised sectarianism: 'key provisions in the [Good Friday] Agreement mark it out as a settlement between national communities rather than ethnic or religious communities' (2004: 10). The issue is ethno-nationalism not sectarianism.

But not any old national communities/subjectivities. Which ones? For Nairn writing in 1977 the problem with protestants was that they had failed to develop an Ulster nationalism. But Ulster nationalism is not what animated the peace process. Rather the peace process was informed by, and sought to cultivate, a national subject who was British or maybe British–Irish, albeit one who was steeped in his/her own culture, preferably defined in terms of the Ulster–Scots language and music, which is more manageable than orange supremacism.

Community relations work and cultural relations programmes are informed by and seek to cultivate the ethno-national subjects appropriate to consociational governmentality. If we have focused on cultivation of politically fragmented northern protestants as British nationalists, it is because this effort appears to have been regarded as being the more difficult one. As Church *et al.* note 'the majority of single-identity projects . . . are found in the protestant/unionist community, which has experienced an increasing sense of alienation as a result of the political reforms stemming from the "peace process"' (2004: 284).[2]

Re-making republicans as ethno-nationalists, does not seem to have been regarded as being quite so problematic. However, we should note the testimony of leading republicans like Kevin Rooney and Anthony McIntyre who are in no doubt that the GFA has involved a makeover of republicans as ethno-nationalists. Rooney says he always rejected media suggestions that the

> political conflict [w]as a sectarian one . . . because I believe . . . that the divisions in Ireland are artificial, created and maintained by Britain to enable it to rule its last colony . . . I was certainly not alone in my rejection of sectarian divisions. Throughout the '80s and early 90s *there was a strong strand in the republican movement that insisted that nationalism and unionism were artificial, political creations and that the goal of a United Ireland was not about a victory of nationalism but the removal of the force that created the material and political basis for the divisions* . . . the Good Friday Agreement has put an end to the prospects for overcoming these divisions and institutionalises the differences between Catholics and protestants. The republicans who espoused the anti-sectarian politics which inspired me, are now at the forefront of demanding laws and institutions that celebrate difference.
>
> (Rooney 1998: 21, my emphasis)

It might be tempting to see the recent growth in the armed activity of dissident republicans as a manifestation of the difficulty of remaking republicans as ethno-nationalists. This would be a mistake. Here we need to make a distinction between republican dissidents like Rooney and McIntyre and the dissident republicans in the Real or Continuity IRAs. Rooney and McIntyre are critical of Sinn Fein's participation in the GFA, but not because they wanted the armed struggle to continue; on the contrary McIntyre is a republican dissident because he feels that Sinn Fein has not been honest about the failure of the armed struggle or the implications of that failure (McIntyre 2008). Neither the Real IRA nor the Continuity IRA dissent from the ethno-national logic of the GFA; arguably, they are militant versions of that logic: what is known in the literature on conflict resolution as outbidders.

Techniques and programmes to cultivate ethno-national subjectivities are familiar enough in the world. We have already mentioned the production of 'national being' in post-Dayton Bosnia-Herzegovina. And one might also think of Russian speakers left high and dry in the Baltic states as the Soviet empire receded. Dace Dzenovska discusses the efforts by the Latvian state to manage 'sovki' or Soviet persons. Sovki are problematic not only because they are representatives of an erstwhile ruling class, but because they lack 'proper ethnic consciousness'; the 'denationalized mass' of

> Russian-speakers, Soviet … immigrants … for whom national belonging was of no great importance . . . These denationalized beings are said to be concerned only with the 'good life' as material well-being, incapable of appreciating the higher goods of life and thus show no interest or ability to learn about and respect the local ways, including learning the Latvian language.
>
> (2006: 5)

The Latvian state has developed programmes that aimed at 'rescuing' sovki from a 'denationalized and thus not fully human existence' (Dzenovska 2006: 6). This theme of the materialistic de-moralisation of the deracinated is resonant: it once formed part of the means whereby Irish nationalists explained unionism and partition (see O'Halloran 1987)[3] and is still used today to condemn those who stray from their communal roots (see McKay 2000).[4]

The programmes developed by the Latvian government are part of what Dzenovska describes as a policy of national multiculturalism. What they share with the programmes that I have described in Northern Ireland and that Mujkic and others have alluded to in Bosnia-Herzegovina is that they are informed by and seek to cultivate proper forms of subjectivity rooted in an ethno-national culture. People who do not perform a proper ethno-national identity are regarded as problematic: deracinated, materialistic and amoral.

Ethnic normalisation and the genealogy of power

The picture that I am developing is of a consociational form of liberal governmentality that normalises the ethnic or the ethno-national through a combination of discipline and programmes that aim to 'produce national being', ethno-national subjects or identities. To bring it into sharper focus we must confront a potential difficulty: programmes that are informed by and seek to foster ethno-national subjectivities give priority to the group rather than the individual, and might therefore be construed as running contrary to or in tension with the main thrust of Foucault's genealogy of power/knowledge. In Foucault's analysis liberal governmentality is predicated on a sociohistorical context in which the individual has choice; that is, is freed from, amongst other things, primordial ties and overweening loyalty to the group. In the afterword to Dreyfus and Rabinow's discussion of his work, Foucault argues:

> power is less a confrontation between two adversaries . . . Than a question of government. This word must be allowed the very broad meaning it had in the sixteenth century. 'Government' did not refer only to political structures or the management of states; rather it designated the way in which the conduct of individuals or of groups might be directed: the government of children, of souls, of communities, of families, of the sick . . . to govern in this sense is to structure the possible field of action of others . . . *Power is exercised only over free subjects, and only insofar as they are free. By this we mean individual or collective subjects who are faced with a field of possibilities in which several ways of behaving, several reactions and diverse comportments may be realized. . . . Slavery is not a power relationship when man is in chains* . . . the relationship between power and freedom's refusal to submit cannot therefore be separated.
>
> (Foucault 1982: 221, my emphasis)

Notwithstanding the reference to 'groups' and 'collective subjects' in the above quote, the main thrust of Foucault's discussion in *Discipline and Punish* and in subsequent discussions of 'pastoral power', is that normalisation in the liberal state is predicated on the unencumbered individual. And yet here am I arguing that consociational is a form of liberal governmentality: a response by the liberal state to conflict in which individual identity is reduced to, or conflated with, communal identity. The latter is understood as being rooted in a shared, inherited culture: one that is vital because it is not something about which we have a choice.

This brings us to one of the main criticisms of Foucault's work: that its emphasis on the individualising character of disciplinary power is symptomatic of his Eurocentricism. Thus, while Foucault's work has been highly influential on postcolonial theory, postcolonial theorists have been among his foremost critics (see Loomba 1998). Their argument is that from a colonial standpoint the genealogy of power looks very different. The genealogy that Foucault presents sometimes seems to be one in which the state becomes less reliant on spectacular forms of punishment and repression, and more reliant on subtle disciplinary and productive practices. This was not the pattern in the colonies, where the former remained the dominant mode. Moreover, while it may be the case that in Europe, disciplinary practices work through the identification of abnormal subjects who stand as a lesson to the normal, this was not the case in the colonies. There, every colonial person is already an abnormal 'other' and the need to single out the madman, the leper, the delinquent, the pervert and so forth is less compelling. Drawing on Vaughan's (1991) study of colonial biomedicine, Loomba concludes:

> the individuation of subjects that took place in Europe was denied colonised people. Colonial medical discourse conceptualised Africans as members of groups 'and it was these groups, rather than individuals, who were said to possess distinctive psychologies and bodies. In contrast to the European developments described by Foucault, in colonial Africa group classification was a far more important construction than individuation'.
>
> (Loomba 1998: 52–53)

Similarly the forms of consociational governmentality with which we are concerned: normalisation through groups and group classification is also more important than individualising strategies.[5]

Reassuring though this might be to our argument, it generates further questions, which though beyond the scope of this book strictly defined, are nevertheless worth registering. One of the aims of this book is to sketch a genealogy of the peace process. This is a modest task; much more modest than, say, offering a genealogy of power in Ireland. From a northern perspective, such a genealogy would need to encompass three periods or epochs: the period prior to independence; the period of the Stormont regime from 1921 to March 1972 when it was 'prorogued' or discontinued; and the period of 'direct rule' from Westminster between March 1972 and the signing of the GFA. How we conceptualise these different epochs – in themselves, in relation to each other and in relation to Ireland's colonial history – has a bearing on themes that concern us greatly: the construction of subject positions and identities and the relationship between different modalities of power.

As we have seen Northern Ireland was established as the largest area in which protestants formed a viable majority. It was in the words of its first Prime Minister, James Craig, conceived as a 'protestant state' in opposition to the 'Catholic state' in the south; a binary opposition that was shared by many in the southern government. The Stormont regime did not seek to assimilate Catholics, rather it constructed them as an internal other. The extent to which this construction of self and other drew on colonial versions of identity was brought home to me a few years ago when I came across the geography textbook passed down to me by sister, which was still at use in the school we both attended in the 1970s (Preece and Wood 1968). It was a state school – complacently protestant – in a suburb of north Belfast. The book was first published in 1938, the edition in my possession is the fifteenth, reprinted in 1968. The book is entitled *The British Isles*. It has fifteen chapters on English regions, three on Scotland, one on Wales and one, the penultimate chapter, on Ireland. This chapter has a section on political divisions that attempts to explain partition. It makes some reference to the troubled history of British/ Irish relations and then says:

> The six counties of Northern Ireland differ from the Irish Republic in having fewer Roman Catholics and more people not of pure Irish lineage, largely due to the 'plantation' of Scottish settlers during the reign of James I. The people of Northern Ireland have many Scottish characteristics, and are more thrifty, far-seeing, and methodical than the more carefree, happy-go-lucky, quick-tempered people of the South.
>
> (1968: 222)

Unable or unwilling to see the possibility that Irish underdevelopment was the product of an unequal colonial relationship, British writers and administrators chose instead to see it as a product of defects in the Irish national character, or cultural identity as we would call it today (Deane 1997). The subjectivities projected in the textbook attest to the staying power of this ideology of progress.

Thus, for all the repressive power at the disposal of the state in Northern Ireland, it would be a mistake to underestimate the role of an ideology of progress and associated modes of subjectivity in galvanising support for partition and its maintenance. Bew *et al.* describe this ideology as being a specific representation of the uneven development of capitalism in Ireland whereby 'the social and economic character of the north, and in particular its monopolisation of capitalist machine industry, was the expression of two distinct *racial* and religious histories . . . It centred on the backward – agrarian/progressive – industrial antithesis' (Bew *et al.* 1979: 8, my emphasis). The effects of this ideology of progress on self-understandings persisted long after de-industrialisation had eroded its material basis; its continued significance is attested to in school textbooks such as my own, and if Liam O'Dowd is correct, in unionism's failure to develop a 'normal' national identity.

It is this lingering effect of colonialism on identity formation that should make us wary of endorsing the politics or recognition inscribed in the GFA. The notion of parity of esteem is based on the idea that cultures – especially

the cultures of oppressed ethnic minorities – require some sort of official recognition if the identity and self-esteem of individuals is not to suffer damage.
As I said in Chapter 4 I do not wish to deny those whose self-understanding
depends on this view of their culture and identity. Nevertheless, it is important
to recognise the slipperiness of identity politics. Anti-imperialist struggles
are often preceded by cultural revivals which seek to liberate a pre-colonial
cultural identity, but 'this identity and the will to assert it are in fact generated
by the situation of oppression' and the danger is that this reinforces domination by condemning the oppressed 'to appeal to the very categories used to
oppress them' (Armstrong 2008: 20). This is what I think Seamus Deane was
getting at when he called for, 'new writing, a new politics, unblemished by
Irishness but securely Irish' (1984). Deane was to become a powerful critic of
cultural policy in Northern Ireland in the late 1980s and 1990s.

The 'troubles' as a state of exception

It was not a cultural or national movement that exposed the 'protestant state'
it was an inter-ethnic *Civil Rights* Movement that demanded equal citizenship for Catholics, only later did a war of national liberation develop: after
the Stormont regime demonstrated its inability to respond adequately or to
control the loyalist reaction. The GFA is an attempt to resolve the impasse.

How do we conceptualise the period in-between, colloquially known as
'the Troubles'? The best answer to this question is given by Arthur Aughey
who described it as a 'state of exception' (2007, 1997), anticipating Georgio
Agamben, who uses the notion of biopower to conceptualise the relationship between liberal democracy and routinised states of emergency (2005).
A state of exception is a period when the rule of law is selectively with-
drawn by the sovereign power. As Judith Butler points out, the application
of Agamben's work to the actions of the United States following 9/11 has
led to a clarification of the relationship between Foucault's notions of sovereignty, disciplinary society and governmentality. These are not 'histori-
cally concrete phenomenon that might be said to succeed each other in time';
rather they are 'modes of conceptualizing power' (2006: 60). The process
whereby United State Government officials unilaterally deemed the people
detained at Guantanamo Bay as a danger to the state is described by Butler
as 'a ghostly and forceful resurgence of sovereignty in the midst of governmentality' (2006: 59).

The description of 'the Troubles' as a state of exception, seems apt in many
ways, not least because it was a period when the sovereign power to repress
was much apparent. Thus, one Irish critic of Foucault, writing of his abuse

at the hands of a British army foot patrol in Belfast in 1993 – that is, early in the peace process and before the ceasefires – emphasises the violence that underpinned routine surveillance:

> I do not mean to imply that power can be reduced to violence or coercion; power can also involve the use of manipulation or authority. Nevertheless, the ability to use force can be seen as the exercise of power in the last instance . . . most Western Governments succeed in ruling by means of a combination of manipulation and authority. However, these modes of political power have not been successful in Ireland, where Britain's jurisdictional authority over the six north-eastern counties has been strenuously challenged. The challenge has had the effect of stripping away the liberal veneer, and exposing the crude physical force that lurks beneath. In doing so, it brings into stark focus the amount of power that even the dregs of an imperial nation can possess and utilize.
>
> (Porter 1996: 66)

Drawing on fieldwork conducted in Belfast between 1984 and 1986, Feldman makes a similar point, albeit with a more subtle understanding of Foucault. Having remarked on the frightening noise made by police and army land rovers in the silence of the early morning, Feldman suggests that,

> arrest in Northern Ireland is thus analogous to Foucault's description of public execution: 'a policy of terror to make everyone aware through the body of the criminal, of the unrestrained presence of the sovereign. The public execution did not re-establish justice; it reactivated power' . . . Arrest as a performative display reactivates the political potency of the state which has been suspended by the 'terrorist' act.
>
> (1991: 89)

We should also note that all throughout the period of 'the Troubles' and continuing for sometime after the ceasefires, loyalist and republican paramilitaries themselves inflicted spectacular forms of punishment of their own devising on dissidents and anti-social elements within their respective communities: symbolic quarterings in which joints are damaged or destroyed rather than sundered.

The peace process marked a transition when the balance between the various forms of power shifted. Some of the more overt manifestations of topdown sovereign power – British army patrols and raids and checkpoints and so forth – have been effaced, and paramilitary rough justice has given way to a more diffused managerial approach:

> The interface areas seem to be moving towards joint Republican-Loyalist management, already germinating from the Sinn Fein meetings with the Loyalist Commission, which knit managerial strata from each camp closer together . . . the nature of the Provisional relationship to the nationalist community has evolved from loosely defending it to a position of tightly controlling it.
>
> (McIntyre 2008: 128)

As O'Broin points out (2008), one of the major successes of the GFA has been the manner in which it has penetrated social worlds and recruited political actors hitherto beyond the reach of most government agencies (see also McVeigh and Rolston 2007). From a Foucauldian point of view, what is significant about the co-management of interface areas by former paramilitaries is that this was not sponsored by the state from above, it was improvised from below. Indeed the dynamic of this informal peace process has often been at variance with the official process (Jarman 2006).

Conclusion

This book is a genealogy of a particular approach to peacemaking that draws on a pluralist political rationality. Focusing on Ireland, this chapter started by arguing that the introduction of a theory of pluralism and cultural identity was a paradigm shift, and showed how this new paradigm was used to make problems legible. Notable here was the 'protestant identity crisis'. We then took a detour into a larger genealogy of power in Ireland. The main purpose of this detour was to highlight the significance of the paradigm shift as not being merely scientific but also programmatic: as a shift in power/knowledge. To the extent that the modes of power and subjectivity that inform the GFA are a break with those bequeathed from an earlier period tainted by a legacy of colonial struggle, then it has got to be a good thing. In this context, ethno-national forms of subjectivity can be seen as potentially more productive than modes of subjectivity rooted in supremacist and racialised notions of progress.

To take one unlikely example. The GFA makes special provision alongside the Irish language for Ulster-Scots language and culture. A significant part of this culture is Scottish dance music. The promotion of this musical form has provided a domesticated, alternative for loyalist flute bands that are traditionally associated with paramilitary displays and an aggressive form of 'kick the Pope' music with sectarian lyrics. According to Gordon Ramsay, Scottish dance, 'jiggy', music played by members of loyalist bands is now featured at a wide-range of social events, even in night clubs (Ramsay 2008).

One might attach a larger significance to the normalising programmes and practices discussed in this and the preceding chapter. As Dreyfus and Rabinow point out, Foucault rejected philosophies of meaning such as hermeneutics and phenomenology because, following Nietzsche, he was mindful of how 'power uses the illusion of meaning to further itself' (1982: xxiii). Normalisation involves making individuals and groups and their actions meaningful. There's a sense in which defining the struggle in Northern Ireland as a national one dignifies it, makes it meaningful and useful in that other places can learn from it. In a 1998 article comparing Northern Ireland and South Africa, John McGarry described the conflict in the former as being 'a quarrel involving two groups who wish to belong to different states'. Drawing on this analysis Aaron Edwards and Stephen Bloomer comment

> Although both groups hold democratic views on constitutional matters, a cutting-edge response has . . . emerged – in the form of paramilitary organisations – in a bid to further these ethno-national goals by force of arms. The *integrity* of the quarrel has meant that any options . . . for a termination of the conflict had to acknowledge . . . armed non-state actors . . . Northern Ireland proves to be a useful model for conflict management.
>
> (2008: 10–11, my emphasis)

Making the conflict meaningful – no longer an anomaly, normalised – it can be used as a model for other places.

7   No exit

Human rights and the priority
of ethnicity

Chastened perhaps by the example of apartheid South Africa, consociational theorists developed the idea that the groups participating in a power-sharing arrangement need not be predetermined, but could and maybe should be self-determining (see Chapters 2 and 3). In practice however consociational governmentality, drawing on certain ideas about communal identity and autonomy, sanctions community programs and community relations techniques that are informed by, valorise and aim to cultivate, individual and collective subjects who understand themselves to be defined by ethno-nationalism (see Chapters 5 and 6). In Chapter 4 we saw that in Northern Ireland, communal designation has become almost ineluctable: not just when filling in a census form or applying for a job but when signing up to a variety of everyday organisations and activities.

And yet, the normalisation of the ethno-national is not complete. People continue to elude the specified ethno-national categories. The GFA and the Dayton Accords made some allowances for this by inventing a special category. In both cases the word used to designate this special category is the same: 'other' and 'Others', respectively. The GFA states, 'At their first meeting, members of the Assembly will register a designation of identity – nationalist, unionist or *other* – for the purposes of measuring cross-community support in Assembly votes under the relevant provisions above' (Strand one 'Democratic Institutions in Northern Ireland'). As an annex to one of its 11 articles, the Dayton Accords states:

> Recalling the Basic Principles agreed in Geneva on September 8, 1995, and in New York on September 26, 1995, Bosniacs, Croats, and Serbs, as constituent peoples (along with *Others*), and citizens of Bosnia and Herzegovina hereby determine that the Constitution of Bosnia and Herzegovina is as follows . . . .
>
> (1995, Annex 4, my emphasis)

The choice of word is literal, but whoever picked it must not have been a student of cultural studies, for in that context, the term 'other' has become shorthand for exclusion, subordination, feminisation or normalisation. Dreyfus and Rabinow present normalisation as an ongoing process that validates itself through the

> systemic creation, classification and control of anomalies in the social body . . . As Foucault has shown . . . in *Discipline and Punish* and the *History of Sexuality* . . . the advance of biopower is contemporary with the appearance and proliferation of the very categories of anomalies – the delinquent, the pervert, and so on – that technologies of power and knowledge were supposedly designed to eliminate. The spread of normalization operates through the creation of abnormalities which it then must treat and reform.
>
> (1982: 195–96)

The abnormal 'other' stands as a lesson to – and is therefore constitutive of – the normal. The other has what might be called 'negative constitutional significance'.

Resisting the temptation to a hasty functionalist interpretation of the significance of the use of the term 'Others'/'other' in the Dayton Accords and the GFA, we should note the signs of contingency. In the Dayton Accords 'Others' is in brackets, which might suggest that it was an afterthought, but the capital 'O' and the context suggests a something definite – a proper noun – almost on a par with the three constituent peoples. By contrast, the lower case 'o' and context in which 'other' is mentioned in the GFA – merely part of the technology for measuring cross-community support in the Assembly – suggests the kind of residual, catchall category beloved of those who design forms and questionnaires.

In this chapter I want to explore the significance of the category 'other'/ 'Others' by examining another key feature of the common technology of peace; that is, human rights. Because of their universalism, the notion that they offer protection to all, including 'others', it is hoped that human rights will act as a unifying mechanism in the aftermath of conflict. In other words, a significant part of the political rationale for human rights provisions in consociational peace agreements is that they can transcend ethnic divisions. For this reason human rights organisations tend to be the first place that people who do not fit the specified categories look for support (e.g. see Langhammer 11 October 2000). This function of human rights is acknowledged by consociationalists. As we noted in Chapter 2, one response to the criticism that the GFA institutionalises sectarianism is to invoke the human rights and equality provisions of the Agreement which offer 'protection to individuals, including those who regard themselves as neither unionist nor nationalist' (McGarry 2001: 122). It is this that makes human rights provision of peace agreements – the Dayton Accord and GFA anyway – strategic when it comes to comprehending the significance of the 'other' category.

The human rights processes initiated by the Dayton Accords and the GFA

Both the GFA and Dayton Accord set in train elaborate human rights processes, formal and informal. The GFA made provision for a Northern Ireland Human Rights Commission (NIHRC), which, among other things was to advise on the scope of a Bill of Rights for Northern Ireland, which would supplement, 'the European Convention on Human Rights, to reflect the particular circumstances of Northern Ireland . . . These additional rights to reflect the principles of mutual respect for the identity and ethos of both communities and parity of esteem' (1998, Strand Three, Rights Safeguards and Equality of Opportunity: 4). As we saw in Chapter 2, the NIHRC's first draft Bill of Rights published in September 2001 was, in the words of the first Chairperson of the NIHRC, 'roundly condemned for not having brought on board the political parties and squared the political circle' (Dickson 2009).

In 2005 a new set of commissioners were appointed under a new Chair, a leading member of the Women's Coalition.[1] In 2006, following the St Andrews Agreement,[2] the Northern Ireland Office established a Bill of Rights Forum consisting of representatives of the political parties, 'civil society', the churches and business and chaired by an international human rights expert. The Forum failed to reach a consensus on the Bill of Rights, and its report, submitted to the NIHRC in March 2008, laid out various and often conflicting options. Even the NIHRC itself was unable to produce an agreed document: two unionist commissioners dissented from the advice the commission presented to the Secretary of State on 10 December 2008.

The 'Preamble' to Annex 4 of the Dayton Accords (1995) states that the constitution of Bosnia-Herzegovina is,

> Inspired by the Universal Declaration of Human Rights, the International Covenants on Civil and Political Rights and on Economic, Social and Cultural Rights, and the Declaration on the Rights of Persons Belonging to National or Ethnic, Religious and Linguistic Minorities, as well as other human rights instruments.

Article II of the Constitution provides that the European Convention on Human Rights 'shall apply directly in Bosnia and Herzegovina' and shall have 'priority over all other law'. Annex 6 provides for a Human Rights Commission consisting of an internationally appointed Ombudsman and a Human Rights Chamber. The former investigates and the latter adjudicates. Unlike the NIHRC, the Human Rights Commission provided for in the Dayton Accords does not have responsibility for developing a Bill of Rights or for consciousness raising. But Annex 6 requires parties to the accords to 'promote and encourage the activities of non-governmental and international organizations for the protection and promotion of human rights' (1995). In both places government involves the promotion of what is now referred to as a 'culture of human rights'.

In both places, the human rights provisions have proved controversial and difficult to implement. Christine Bell explains the difficulties as follows: 'the implementation of human rights measures is largely dependent on some type of meta-bargain having been reached', but this bargain has not been secured in either Bosnia-Herzegovina or Northern Ireland. With regard to Northern Ireland, 'the bargain is incomplete [for] the agreement is compatible with both British unionist and Irish nationalist sovereign aspirations for the future'. Thus in opposing the NIHRC's final advice to the Secretary of State some unionists argued that the human rights process in Northern Ireland be subsumed into a broader United Kingdom process.[3] With regard to Bosnia-Herzegovina, Bell argues that, in the text of Dayton 'it is clear . . . that the human rights institutions which aim to cement the unitary state stand at odds with the entities and the scope of their autonomy' and 'given the lack of ethno-national consent to the unitary structure it is not surprising that there is resistance to implementing the decisions of the human rights institutions' (Bell 2000: 299).

In the absence of a meta-bargain having been reached, the danger is that human rights becomes a new terrain on which the old conflicts are fought. This is what the 'liberal' critique of consociation as the institutionalisation of division might lead us to expect: the danger is of what Robin Whitaker calls 'the communalization of rights' (2010: 26). In both places there are tendencies in this direction.

A recent report on civil society actors and human rights promotion in Bosnia-Herzegovina conducted by the Oslo International Peace Research Institute and the Marburg University's Center of Conflict Studies concludes that most human rights organisations are 'active only in their own entity (Federation or Republika Srpska) without communication among one another'(Marcon *et al.* 2008: 26) and that some Bosnian civil society organisations seek to promote human rights 'for the persons of their own ethnic group' and only a 'few' have 'tried to promote a real reconciliation among the different communities and to work at state level and not only in their own entity' (2008: 27). Against this I met with the members of several organisations that were based in Sarajevo, but whose social and ethnic composition was mixed and which either worked across the whole of Bosnia-Herzegovina or had sister organisations in other entities. I did encounter disillusionment among some of the human rights activists I met, but this had various sources, not least the actions of 'the international community'.

In Northern Ireland there is clear unionist and nationalist disagreement about the provisions of the most recent draft Bill of Rights. The major division is that the former preferred a minimalist Bill of Rights, one that was bound tightly to the particular circumstances of Northern Ireland narrowly defined and to the principle of parity of esteem, ethos and identity, while the latter supported a Bill of Rights that addressed Northern Ireland's social and economic circumstances as well as its civil and political ones. The former chair of the NIHRC sums up unionist objections as follows

> What really irks many unionists – though it may also displease nationalists when the crunch comes – is that the proposed Bill will allow NGOs and others to go to court and claim that government ministers . . . are not progressing towards full realisation of the rights to health, an adequate standard of living, work and social security. The commission has adopted an all-guns-blazing approach to social and economic rights, beyond even what South Africa, Finland, and Hungary, the supposed leaders in the field, have opted for.
>
> (Dickson 2009: 11)

Whitaker concludes her analysis of the debates and controversy by arguing against the idea that it can be characterised in terms of 'communalization of rights':

> NIHRC's interpretation of its mandate (consultation, monitoring and advice; public information and education) created spaces for people and groups to pursue a wide range of agendas, articulate diverse hopes and fears, and fire salvos. As much as competing nationalities, debate has been about competing social models, competing ideas of democracy and competing philosophies of rights, none of which are merely local. Nor do the disputants resolve neatly into Catholics/nationalists, Protestants/unionists and others. A closer look reveals multiple differences, not only

between groups or even within them, but also within individual members of those groups.[4]

(2010: 38)

While it would not be accurate to describe the human rights processes initiated by the Dayton Accords and the GFA as the communalisation of rights, it is nevertheless true that they have not succeeded in one of their main official purposes; that is, acting as a unifying force. This difficulty could have been anticipated. There were early signs, and Christopher McCrudden, a leading advocate of consociation warned that, 'establishing the appropriate relationships between international human rights law and consociational arrangements is likely to be a complex interpretative task' (2006: 3). And yet huge resources and large hopes continued to be invested in human rights processes. One wonders why? Beyond inertia, there is the Foucauldian question: if the human rights processes set in train by the GFA and the Dayton Accords have not achieved their ostensible purposes what is served by their failure? What are the outcomes?

Outcomes of the human rights processes initiated by the Dayton Accords

In both Bosnia-Herzegovina and Northern Ireland, running alongside arguments about whose rights and which rights are to be protected, there has been another more fundamental argument going on about the nature of rights as such. We touched on this in Chapters 2 and 3. This is the argument about whether rights are a property of individuals or of groups or of both; and if both, which should have priority. In practical terms the argument boils down to whether human rights instruments in Northern Ireland and Bosnia-Herzegovina should include provision for a right to self-identification or, to be more specific, a right of exit from the communities and peoples specified in the peace agreements.

Summarising the debate in Bosnia-Herzegovina, Edin Hodžić, formerly of the research and analysis section of the Office of the Prosecutor, contrasts the richness of the Dayton human rights provisions and the poverty of their implementation. He notes,

the absolute domination of continued debate on the conflict between individual and collective rights in the constitutional and legal order of BiH (Bosnia-Herzegovina), which has been going on, with alterable intensity, practically from the moment the Dayton Agreement was signed

... [and] continues to revolve persistently around one or two poles in this already quite predictable debate. On the one hand, the abstract citizen is insisted upon as the only genuine holder of rights, while on the other side, there are opposing approaches based on absolutism and supreme authority of ethnic communities.

He implies that the persistent recurrence of this debate is intrinsic to consociation:

we are deeply entrenched in a consociation model. Almost by definition, the consociation model, implies a continued state of crisis, be it realistic or construed. The crisis, in fact, is the way of political life, while finding mechanisms for its overcoming is the essence of actions of all participants in the political arena.

And he bemoans the fate of Bosnia-Herzegovina as a kind of test-case, watched closely by the international community to see if it can achieve what has so far eluded everyone else; that is, 'deliver guidelines for innovation of rigid solutions provided by the paradigms of liberalism or consocialism' (Hodžić 5 July 2006).

Those who query the supremacy of ethnic groups and argue that human rights should accrue to us as individuals are regarded with suspicion or skepticism. This was brought home to me at a conference dinner in Sarajevo. The keynote speaker had given a talk earlier in the day in which he had elaborated a contrast between the vitality of communalist politics and the enervation of politics in the liberal state. The audience at the lecture had queried what appeared to be his endorsement of communalism and those members of the audience who came to dinner continued the discussion. While that was going on, I was chatting to our dinner-host, the conference organiser. I told him about the debacle of the first draft Bill of Rights in Northern Ireland, and speculated as to why individual rights seemed to be asserted with more confidence in Bosnia-Herzegovina. Was it to do with the role in Bosnia-Herzegovina of international NGOs captivated by the romance of Sarajevo's multi-ethnic history and the tragedy of its destruction? Was it to do with the recentness of communist, one-party rule (see Helsinki Human Rights 2005a)? No, no, he said and invited me to look around the dinner table. There were five people aside from myself, the visiting speaker and our host. All five were Bosniaks, he said, explaining that Bosniaks are a majority in Bosnia-Herzegovina and feel more confident about a unitary state in which rights would accrue to individual citizens.

The tone of the dinner-host was affectionate, but in other contexts to challenge the priority accorded to the ethnic group over the individual can provoke a severe reaction, one that is licensed by the perpetual sense of crisis that Hodžić alludes to. Mujkic argues that in the 'ethnopolis' where 'taking part in politics takes the form of obeying a biological obligation', the 'notion of the individual citizen, abstracted from his ethnic and religious kinship, is viewed as subversive'. To be 'other' in this sense is to be guilty of 'a despicable' we might add dubious 'form of atheism, moral corruption, decadence, and rebellion' (2007: 120). As evidence he cites the 'Stalinesque' rhetoric of those 'ethnopoliticians' who accused a group of social democratic politicians, journalists, and intellectuals of attempting coup d'état in 2003. The charges were dropped, but normalisation does not depend on a successful prosecution (Foucault 2007: 56).

Outcomes of the human rights processes initiated by the GFA

Part of the function of human rights processes in the aftermath of conflict is pedagogical and inspirational: fostering a 'culture of human rights'. It is fitting therefore that large questions should be aired about the nature of rights and what it means to be human. There have been moments when the debate in Northern Ireland has been like this. Early in the debate surrounding the first draft Bill of Rights, supporters of the idea that there should be a right of exit invited international experts to participate in local discussions. Supporters of the idea that groups have rights invoked existential arguments about the importance of communal identity to individual identity, referred to larger debates concerning the politics of recognition, and appealed to renowned authorities such as Charles Taylor (1994), Will Kymlicka (1995) and so forth (e.g. see Harvey 2003: 90).

Gradually the public debate became inflected by a note of crisis and, with that, increasingly technocratic. 'Academic' discussion was denounced (see Russell 2004). The clearest exposition of the technocratic case against allowing the individual to have a right *not* to be treated as a member of one or other of the two communities specified in the GFA is articulated by Christopher McCrudden:

> the concept of consociationalism adopted and incorporated by the [Good Friday] Agreement include those provisions of the Agreement that established particular voting procedures in the legislature, and also those domestic anti-discrimination and equality policies that addressed economic disparities between Catholics and Protestants in

employment . . . Although the latter predated the Agreement, it was under-pinned by the Agreement. The important connection between the two is not only that, however, but also that both rely, to some extent on using group identity as an important element in the way they are operationalized.

(2007: 317)[5]

Group identity is a vital mechanism used to operationalise both voting procedures in the local legislature and procedures for monitoring the communal composition of workforces and job applicants (see Chapter 4). To include provision for a right of exit in the Bill of Rights would be to expose this vital mechanism to legal challenge. The nature of identity and rights are no longer issues of existential, moral, political and philosophical issues of legitimate concern to all, but a technical issue and technical issues are the preserve of those with the requisite technical training and expertise, in this case legal training/expertise.

As an architect of equality legislation McCrudden is particularly concerned with the potential impact of a right of exit on employment monitoring procedures. He argues that the introduction of these procedures in the early 1990s was vexed and that to reopen the issue years later in the context of debate about the Bill of Rights is 'close to irresponsible' (2007: 341). In an article written shortly before publication of the second draft Bill of Rights, McCrudden raised the temperature further by arguing that a legal challenge to employment monitoring procedures arising from a right of exit would be 'destabilizing' (2008: 8).

This invocation of crisis seems excessive (see Chapter 4; see also Hadden 2008). And it is not at all clear why one could not have a Bill of Rights that acknowledged a right of exit, while ensuring that fair employment monitoring could continue unimpaired. Indeed, during the debate on the first draft Bill of Rights, a whole range of organisations advocated this position; including the Irish Congress of Trade Unions, the Northern Ireland Council for Voluntary Action and the Northern Ireland Women's Coalition (Whitaker 2010).

Nevertheless, McCrudden's arguments seem to have had the desired effect. In the Human Rights Forum established in 2006, Sinn Fein and the Social Democratic and Labour Party voiced their opposition to a right of exit. The unionist parties were unenthusiastic. The Alliance Party was alone in continuing to argue for a right of exit based on Article 3(1) of the European Framework Convention on the Protection of National Minorities. Article 3(1) states that:

Every person belonging to a national minority shall have the right to freely choose to be treated or not to be treated as such and no disadvantage shall result from this choice or from the exercises of the rights which are connected to that choice.

(Council of Europe 1995)

Alliance argued that the protection that the Framework Convention extends to minorities should be extended to all communities:

> Alliance believes that Northern Ireland is a complicated society with multiple identities, and cross-cutting cleaves. Cultural and identity rights should apply to all persons belonging to different sections of society. Minorities are not fixed, and majorities in one context can be minorities in another . . . The right to self identification is an absolutely critical issue for the Alliance Party. People should be free to identify themselves, and to have this right respected by public authorities . . . Where there are implications for approaches to [fair employment] monitoring, then policies need to be reconsidered. Alliance is opposed to any limitation paragraph on this right.
>
> (Report of the Bill of Rights Forum 2008: 74)

This argument is consistent with that of the Standing Advisory Commission on Human Rights (SACHR) who, as discussed in Chapter 3, introduced the notion of equality of esteem (see Chapter 3 and SACHR 1990: 90).[6] Nevertheless it left the Alliance Party open to the suggestion that it was pursuing some kind of majoritarian agenda. Thus the 'The Human Rights NGO sector' in the Forum argued against the Alliance position, explaining that it had:

> fundamental reservations about . . . the manner in which rights of a minority are treated as synonymous with rights of a community. The term 'minorities' has a specific connotation in international human rights law. The protection of rights is obviously in the interests of everyone in society, whether one is a member of a minority or a majority community. Moreover, the rights of individuals to be protected from discrimination is obviously very important: men, white people, English speakers, heterosexuals, settled people must clearly be protected from discrimination, and must be allowed, like everyone else, to express their identity in private and in society. Special provision is rarely, if ever, however required to ensure protection for such groups – and the elaboration of *the rights of 'dominant' or 'majority' groups* do not figure in international human rights texts. The purpose of minority rights protections is to protect the

most vulnerable groups in society, precisely because they are minority groups. It is quite unacceptable to undermine any of the rights that minority communities have as a result of the Framework Convention.

(Bill of Rights Forum Report 2008: 75–76, my emphasis)

As in Bosnia-Herzegovina, so in Northern Ireland: to advocate a right to self-identification is to lay oneself open to suspicion of pursuing a covert majoritarian agenda. Recall Chapter 2 where we discussed how Alliance Party and the Women's Coalition Members of the Local Assembly relinquished their designation as 'other' to secure the reinstatement of First Minister and Deputy First Minister. Under protest, Alliance members of the Assembly had re-designated themselves as unionist to ensure that their votes would be counted. One might have expected them to have been applauded for helping to save the legislature. On the contrary as Malachi O'Doherty observed at the time:

> There is a whisper of contempt for the Alliance Party being so precious about this move [re-designating as unionist]. It is being said, sure they are unionists anyway and it costs them nothing. What right have they then to be setting terms for acknowledging for a day what they really are?
>
> (2001)

O'Doherty is pointing to the suspicion that by claiming to be 'other', members of the Alliance Party are not being true to themselves. Their pursuit of a right of exit is therefore misguided or dishonest. Worse than that, in the wake of the recent human rights debate, arguing for a right of exit is revealed as being subversive of hard-won equality legislation aimed at redressing generations of discrimination against Catholics in Northern Ireland.

In its final advice to the Secretary of State the NIHRC interpreted the principle of parity of esteem as to require 'the due recognition of the identity, ethos and aspirations of the two main communities in Northern Ireland' (2008: 10). Consistent with this, the 'Culture and Identity' section of the draft Bill of Rights included 'an obligation on public authorities to respect the identity and ethos of both communities' (2008: 98). But the NIHRC also recognised that 'the rights and needs of others must be protected' (2008: 10). How were the rights of others to be protected? Not through the inclusion of a right of exit or a right to self-identification, but by extending protection from the 'two main communities' to 'other linguistic, cultural and ethnic minorities' (2008: 98 and 41).[7] All difference is welcome so long as it's ethnic!

I am minded of Hardt and Negri's prescient observation about the emergence of a 'pluralism' that insists that 'all cultural identities are equal' and 'accepts all the differences of what we are so long as we agree to act on the basis of these differences of identity, so long as we agree to act our race' (2000: 192).

Conclusion

The objectives of the human rights processes inscribed in the Dayton Accords and the GFA are the same as human rights everywhere. But in the specific context of consociational peace agreements with their emphasis on segmental or cultural autonomy, human rights provisions have a vital additional role; that is, to act as a unifying force – one of the few – protecting all the people, including those who do not fit the specified ethno-national categories (see Bell 2000 and McGarry 2001: 122).

In this regard, whatever else they have achieved, the human rights processes provided for in the GFA and the Dayton Accords have not been successful. Rather than acting as a unifying force, human rights processes have been sources of ongoing tension and pseudo-crisis. The old 'liberal' critique of consociation which complains about the institutionalisation of ethnic division might lead us to expect this: that human rights would become a new terrain upon which old communal conflicts are fought out, what Whitaker (2010) calls the communalisation of rights. But as she points out in the case of Northern Ireland, the difficulties and tensions revealed in the deliberations over a Bill of Rights cannot be understood by reducing it to communal standpoints, the debate has been more nuanced than that.

The problem with the human rights processes enacted in Northern Ireland and Bosnia-Herzegovina is that far from transcending ethnicity they have inadvertently served to confirm its overweening importance. And so the most recent draft of the Bill of Rights for Northern Ireland extends recognition from 'the two main communities' to 'other linguistic, cultural and ethnic minorities'. In itself, this extension is very welcome for 'post-conflict' Northern Ireland continues to witness a vicious cultural racism directed against travellers and migrants.[8] Nevertheless, it is worth pointing out that such recognition is not extended to the identities of those who define themselves other than in ethnic terms.

Bosnia-Herzegovina has more well-established ethnic minorities than Northern Ireland, and efforts to secure their recognition have been long-running. After intervention of the High Representative in 2002, 'a number of seats were reserved in the entity parliaments for those not belonging to the constituent peoples' (HCHR 2005b). Also worth noting is the campaign to open up the presidency and the House of Peoples to members of ethnic groups other than the specified constituent peoples. Under the Dayton constitution,

Bosnia has three Presidents representing each of the constituent peoples, and only members of these constituent peoples can run for the presidency. The Minority Rights Group has sponsored an application to the European Court of Human Rights aimed at opening up the presidency to ethnic minorities: Sejdic and Finci vs Bosnia and Herzegovina (application numbers: 27996/06 and 34836/0). Dervo Sejdic is a member of the Roma community, and Jakob Finci a member of the Jewish community. The Minority Rights Group emphasises Finci's ethnic credentials as the leader of Sarajevo's 'small Jewish community whose family has lived in the city for over 300 years . . . the Bosnian constitution is a modern day creation, but de facto reinforces centuries-old discrimination . . . There are about 500 Jews living in Bosnia-Herzegovina' (Minority Rights Group 2006).

Aside from a formal willingness to entertain ethnic others, another similarity between post-peace agreement Bosnia-Herzegovina and Northern Ireland is that in both places non-ethnic 'others' are met with scepticism and worse. At best they are perceived as self-deluded; at worst as dishonest proxies for some kind of majoritarian agenda (Mujkic 19 November 2007). Either way, they are untrue to their innermost selves, and being true to one's innermost self, which in ethnopolis is always one's ethnic self, is the highest virtue. Non-ethnic 'others' are dangerous and subversive, which is presumably why they are sometimes met with an anger that is surprisingly vehement. Whatever underlies the opprobrium, it certainly serves to normalise the ethnic.

If anything, the normalising pressure in Northern Ireland is greater than in Bosnia-Herzegovina. The form of consociation laid out in the Dayton Accords may be defined as corporate and the GFA as liberal, but it is in Northern Ireland that legislation allows for people socialised locally to be categorised as belonging to one or other of the specified ethno-national groups irrespective of how they choose to identify themselves. As the trajectory of the debate on a Northern Ireland Bill of Rights shows, the official reluctance to allow a right of exit from one's supposed community of origin has stiffened in the years since the GFA was signed. In Bosnia-Herzegovina self-identification is allowed despite evidence of abuse by ethnic parties: to do anything else, says Florian Beiber, would not be 'appropriate from the point of view of individual human rights' (2006: 24).

Far from transcending ethnicity the human rights process enacted in Northern Ireland and Bosnia-Herzegovina confirm its overweening importance. Far from protecting people who do not conform to the ethno-national norm, human rights processes in Northern Ireland and Bosnia-Herzegovina have served to confirm their anomalous status.

8 'A long way to get very little'

The durability of identity, socialist politics and communal discipline

There has been some effort in post-conflict Northern Ireland and Bosnia-Herzegovina to recognise ethnicities other than those specified in the peace agreements, but there seems to be a stubborn resistance, considerably more pronounced in the former than the latter, to concede anything on the assumption that indigenes must belong to one or other of the identity categories specified in the respective peace agreements. But how so? It's not because these identities are primordial. Consociationalists have become leery of primordialism. As we have seen McGarry and O'Leary assert that there is a major difference between recognising that ethnic identities are durable and suggesting that they are primordial (2004: 32). But what is the difference? If identities are not primordial, how are they maintained, reproduced and passed on?

In the case of Bosnia-Herzegovina, Paddy Ashdown offers the thought that it is the enmity generated by war that makes ethnic identities perdure. Conflict begets ethnicity rather than the other way round (see also Nic Craith 2002: 15). In the case of Northern Ireland, advocates of liberal consociation no longer even attempt an explanation for the apparent durability of ethnicity. Ignoring decades of anthropological work on ethnic identity by Frederik Barth (1969, see Chapter 3) and others, they simply shrug their shoulders and assert 'that's how it is' or 'it was always thus'.

Here are two quotes to illustrate the exasperated invocation of this supposed historical reality. McGarry (2001: 123) claims that unlike their corporatist cousins, liberal consociationalists are not in favour of 'privileging a particular group of members or pre-determining beneficiaries in advance of elections . . . even if, as in this case [Northern Ireland], the pre-determined groups have constituted almost all the electorate for the past century'. Rejecting the claims of integrationist critics of consociation as 'utopian and mistaken' McGarry and O'Leary argue that 'for over a century historic

Ulster, and then the Northern Ireland that was carved from it, has been divided electorally into two rival ethno-national blocs, the divisions have become particularly intense during the past thirty years' (2004: 19).

This is a large generalisation that masks ideological struggles within, and the changing social composition of the two electoral blocs. It is also to overstate the significance of elections in a polity constituted precisely to ensure that elections were a foregone conclusion. Thus it brackets-out social movements such as the Civil Rights Movement that are neither ethno-national nor concerned with contesting elections. And it diminishes the significance of political parties that sought electoral support from both sides of the sectarian divide, albeit with limited and uneven success. We have discussed the treatment of the Women's Coalition and the Alliance Party. This chapter looks at the way other cross-communal political parties have figured in recent debates about the adequacy of consociation and the GFA. These are the labourist or socialist parties – notably the Northern Ireland Labour Party (NILP) – which contested elections in various shapes and forms from the foundation of Northern Ireland until the mid 1980s (Edwards 2007a and 2007b; Swan 2008; O'Leary 2008).

One might expect that discussion of the socialist past would feature in post-Dayton Bosnia-Herzegovina. For example the strength with which individual rights are asserted is not simply a rejection of ethnopolitics but owes something to the collectivism of the former Yugoslavia and to the cold war origins of some of the human rights organisations active in the region. It is also worth noting that the critics of the Dayton Accords who point to pre-war inter-communal mixing and solidarity are denounced as Yugo-nostalgic.

It is not surprising to find the socialist past, and interpretations of it, invoked in arguments about the Dayton Accords, but who would have thought that labour history would feature in the retrospective justification of the GFA? My purpose in looking at Irish labour history is not to attack consociationalism by demonstrating moments of success for cross-community politics based on common class-interest. Rather, labour history is of interest here as an illustration of the way historical truth-claims are used both to support and to contest the political rationality upon which consociationalism is based; namely the relative weight accorded in explanations of conflict to ethnicity as opposed to class or an 'exaggerated materialism' (O'Leary 2008). Beyond that, and most importantly, I am interested in what the experience of people active in the labour movement in the 1940s, 1950s and 1960s might tell us about communal identities, how they change and perdure. (Before we begin, however, we should register the anachronism in posing the question of identity in regard to a generation for whom the term 'identity' as we use it today would have been quite foreign.)

Labour politics and consociation: a challenge or the exception that proves the rule?

Commenting on 'the heat generated by debate over consociation and its "liberal" or "illiberal" normative trappings', Edwards takes issue with the consociationalist denial of the 'capacity by individual actors to *transform* their social and political identities into something other than merely protestant unionist and Catholic Nationalist' (2007a: 139–40, my emphasis). As an example of this capacity to change he suggests the case of NILP:

> there have been many cases where *transforming* one's identity into something distinct from the prevailing norms can make a measured impact on the political front. The post-war successes of bi-confessional parties, like the democratic socialist Northern Ireland Labour Party, and, from 1970, its liberal Alliance Party successor in transcending these strong ethno-national group identities did make a significant impact.
>
> (2007a: 140, my emphasis)

The NILP secured four seats at Stormont in 1958 and again in 1962, when it got 26 per cent of the total vote, which was its electoral highpoint (Edwards 2009: 72).

Those, like Edwards, who mention the electoral successes of the NILP in the late 1950s and 1960s have been subject to swift and sharp correction by consociationalists (e.g. see Feeney 2009). O'Leary has returned to the issue in a recent review of a book by Paul Bew. What's at issue in this review is not only the malleability or otherwise of identity, but the integrity of consociational rationality. Bew, any more than Edwards, does not dispute the theory that the Northern Ireland conflict is ethno-national, but still they are suspect. The whole point of O'Leary's discussion of Bew's book is to chart the author's apostasy: Bew has moved from an early attachment to Marxist class analysis (Bew *et al.* 1979) to an implicit endorsement of consociationalism; from Louis Althusser to Arend Lijphart, or, as O'Leary puts it, from LA to AL!

O'Leary acknowledges that 'support for the NILP existed in the late 1950s and early 1960s' and that it had a 'moderately high vote share' on occasion. But the thrust of his argument is to deny the significance that Bew once attached, and Edwards would still attach, to the NILP's success. He contests the younger Bew's insistence (with co-authors Gibbon and Patterson, 1979) that, secular and progressive forces were dominant within the protestant working class in the 1960s; [that] a large proportion of the protestant working class were 'not the dupes of Orangeism . . . but were influenced by a secular ideology of opposition to regional deprivation, articulated by the NILP'.

(O'Leary 2008, unpaginated)

Against this, O'Leary asserts the enduring importance of ethnicity over class. The younger Bew exaggerated the significance of the vote for the NILP in the 1960s, says O'Leary:

the NILP's core support in Belfast came predominantly from Catholics – suggesting that working class Catholics were more socialist than working class protestants, though Catholic support for the NILP probably owed more to its role as a parliamentary opponent of the Ulster Unionist Party. When offered a choice between nationalists and the NILP, Catholics preferred the former, and most Catholics were never likely to transfer their loyalties en masse to the NILP because the party, while less prejudiced than the UUP, was, after all, unionist, and, from 1949, solidly pro-partition. The NILP had little to say about Catholic grievances about discrimination, favoured strong measures against the IRA, and its leadership had a strong protestant cultural ethos. Two of its four Stormont MPs elected in 1958 were protestant lay preachers. The party split over the (protestant) issue of Sunday closing in 1965. The protestants who supported the NILP were never dominant in unionist politics.

(O'Leary 2008)

In short, notwithstanding its ability to attract electoral support and members from within the nationalist community, the NILP was not just a unionist party, but an ethnic protestant party. On this reading to invoke the history the NILP is – like Yugo-nostalgia – to smooth over a far from perfect past. And far from innocent, for Slobodan Milosevic used Yugo-nostalgia as a proxy for Serbian Nationalism (see Jansen 2000: 194).

Edwards does not dispute that the NILP in the 1950s was a unionist party, but he does introduce an interesting ambiguity regarding its ethnic character. Sometimes he describes the NILP as an 'inter-ethnic political force' (2009: 227), that is, an alliance between leftists whose ethnicity remained intact. Sometimes he suggests that NILP was transcendent: 'above all the NILP represented a genuine attempt by protestants and Catholics to pursue common class interests *above and beyond ethnic and religious* ones. This . . . is an anomaly worth investigating further' (2009: 4, my emphasis; see also 163). But Edwards also occasionally edges towards the possibility that the NILP was both these things; in other words that it contained within its ranks an admixture of people who had a variable relationship with the unionist and nationalist communities, and included people who regarded themselves as Christian socialists as well as people who regarded themselves secular atheists.

The significance of this last possibility grows if we regard the NILP not simply as a political party whose sole raison d'être was to contest elections, but as part of a broader labour movement. I will expand on this point in the next section. I should stress that my point in doing so is not to counterpoise class to ethnicity as an explanatory variable – the latter was obviously the more compelling for most, most of the time – but to point up the experience of those who actively sought to step outside the communal scripts in the name of socialism and communism.

'Identity' change and the labour movement

The NILP became a unionist party in January 1949 when it declared in favour of partition, prior to that it had been ambiguous. The declaration had been coming for some time, but the immediate circumstances are significant. In December 1948 the Irish President signed the legislation declaring the South of Ireland to be a republic. In January 1949, the nationalist parties in the South joined together to establish a fund raising campaign to finance anti-partition candidates in the North (Farrell 1980: 184). Jack Macgougan, who had been chairman of the NILP 1945–46, described the situation as follows: 'The chapel gate collection', as the anti-partition fund was called, 'led to absolute hysteria in Northern Ireland . . . There's no describing it . . . [it was what] I saw in response to the Anglo-Irish Agreement [1985] doubled or trebled' (interview conducted by Dick Hunter, 5 December 1985[1]).

Macgougan was the leading member of a group of anti-partitionists who had been expelled by the NILP in 1948 and went on to form a northern section of the Irish Labour Party early in 1949. Here's how Michael Farrell, one of the few historians to have dealt with this episode in any detail (see also Walker 1984; Finlay 1989), describes the development of a partitionist NILP:

> The break-up of the Labour Party over the partition issue had shown once again, as in 1920 and 1935 though on a smaller scale, how easily a fragile working class unity built up on social and economic issues, but ignoring, or ambiguous about, the constitutional question, could be

fragmented when the basic existence of state came to the fore. The bulk of the protestant members of the Labour Party retreated toward the unionist camp. As before a small but significant group of protestant radicals went the whole way and joined the anti-partitionist ranks, but just as the events which decide them were not as dramatic as those of 1919 or 1932–33, so they didn't go as far and they became neither Republicans nor Communists, but left-wing members of the Irish Labour Party.

(1980: 196)

Farrell's analysis would appear to confirm the consociational position about the weight of ethno-nationalism and the durability of ethno-national identities as against materialism and class interest. We will return to this in the next section. For the moment, I want to draw your attention to what Farrell's analysis implies about identity-change. He presents the decision of Macgougan and his colleagues to join the Irish Labour Party as transformative. In 1976 when the first edition of Farrell's book was published, identity was not yet the dominant idiom of social and political analysis, but 'identity-change' as it would be called today is what he is getting at: the former members of the NILP who established the Northern Section of the Irish Labour Party were protestants who went 'the whole way' and became something else: anti-partitionist.

The same kind of thinking colours Edward's history of the NILP in the 1950s and 1960s. He uses that history to question the consociationalist's denial of the 'capacity by individual actors to *transform* their social and political identities into something other than merely protestant unionist and Catholic Nationalist' (2007: 140, my emphasis). In this way Edwards bolsters consociational rationality even as he attacks it.

Transformation or conversion is one of the dominant ways in which identity change is coming to be understood in the academic literature.[2] It is consistent with the scientific sectarianism or cultural pluralism discussed in Chapter 4: in Northern Ireland you have to be one thing or the other. Conversion is understood to take place because of some kind of crisis – a catalytic event or events. Farrell, a kind of Alain Badiou (2007) *avant la lettre*, locates the events of 1949 in a sequence of crises that episodes of working class unity provoked for the ruling class. The others he mentions are 1919 and 1932. The former was the occasion of strike by engineering workers in Belfast; the latter was a strike by workers employed on relief schemes aimed at alleviating unemployment. Both strikes were followed by sectarian riots and ethnic cleansings.

We will return to these events in a moment, but before moving on we should note more recent versions of this view of identity-change as conversion or transformation. Todd *et al.* (2006), drawing on interviews carried out at intervals between 1988 and 2006, discuss various kinds of identity change. Overall, they conclude that 'essentializing change' – that is, change that results in a hardening of ethnic identity – is the most common. It occurs as 'an immediate reaction which asserts personal and collective dignity in situations were it is denied' whether through 'institutional injustice' and/or 'collective stigmatization' (2006: 340). They describe 'category change' as rare and 'crisis-ridden' responses to specific events (2006: 338), examples mentioned include

> Alienation from nationalism and Irish identity provoked by encounters with rough, aggressive republican supporters during the 1981 hunger strikes; alienation from the entire British vs. Irish and protestant vs. Catholic binaries provoked by a stabbing by a neighbourhood paramilitary; alienation from unionism provoked by the experience of local 'ethnic cleansing'.
>
> (Todd *et al.* 2006: 338)

Another kind of event thought to have the power to prompt change is spending time outside the country (see Hyndman 1996).

To return to labour history, the point I wish to make is that if you look at the life-histories of people like Jack Macgougan, founder member of the northern section of the Irish Labour Party, you find that they do not conform to this conversion story. Macgougan was born, grew up and lived as an adult in a protestant area of East Belfast. His mother was a Methodist, but he recalled no discernable religious atmosphere at home. His father was an official in the Amalgamated Engineering Union and acted as Election agent for Jack Beattie, a strongly anti-partitionist labour politician who topped the poll for East Belfast in the 1925 Stormont election, was re-elected for Pottinger 1929–43 and elected MP for West Belfast at Westminster 1943–45.

Jack Macgougan described himself as a 'socialist . . . with a national outlook' (interview conducted by Dick Hunter, 15 November 1985). He refused the notion that he came to this position via a 'road to Damascus' conversion, presenting it instead as something that grew out of his milieu. Influenced by reading Jack London, Upton Sinclair and Sholakov thanks to the local public library, the 'left Book club' and Davy McLean's Progressive Bookshop (Devine 1989: 114–115).[3] He also mentioned the Clarion Cycling and Rambling Clubs and the pioneering adult education provided by the National Council of Labour Colleges (which later became the Workers Education Association). As a boy Macgougan helped his father campaign for Beattie. Commenting on Macgougan's 'anti-imperialist' outlook, Devine says that for Macgougan there were simply no 'compelling counter traditions within the Belfast Labour movement' during his formative years in the 1930s. William Walker, a leading member of the labour movement at the turn of century who had opposed home rule for Ireland, was an irrelevance to Macgougan as he came into politics.

Macgougan' s personal development took place in the context of a social movement that in addition to the cultural institutions and influences that he mentions, included a shifting constellation of political parties: the Independent Labour Party, the Socialist Party of Northern Ireland, the Socialist Republican Party, the Northern section of the Irish Labour Party, and the Revolutionary Workers Groups (which became the Communist Party of Ireland), even some early Trotskyists (Milotte 1984). This was a movement that occasionally came together in various permutations to support the struggles of unemployed people, striking workers and particular causes such as the Spanish Civil War (see Malachy Gray 1986: 112). Later on, in the 1950s, partly as a result of the efforts of Macgougan and others like him, there was an all-Ireland trade union centre to which were affiliated all of the local branches of trade unions, some of which had headquarters in Dublin and others in London.

Macgougan was an exceptional figure, but not untypical. Looking at the life histories of some of the other leading members of the labour movement in the 1940s, 1950s, and 1960s, there is no question but that they considered themselves to be socialists or communists and that to be a socialist or a communist was to be something other than a unionist or a nationalist, a protestant or a Catholic. Take Betty Sinclair who chaired the Northern Ireland Civil Rights Association in its early days. Born in a loyalist part of North Belfast, she gravitated from the Labour Party to the newly formed Revolutionary Workers Groups and was a founder member of the Communist Party of Ireland. Sinclair's mother was a Methodist. Her father was not politically active, but he was agnostic and forbade his children from going 'out to the bonfires or sing any of the so-called orange songs': he was, according to Sinclair's biographer, 'a representative of a certain working class type in Belfast whose class interest made him suspicious of dominant ideologies' (Morrissey 1983: 121).

As similar point has been made recently with regard to David Ervine who played an important role in the peace process as leader of the working class loyalist Progressive Unionist Party. Prior to joining the Progressive Unionist Party, Ervine had been active in the paramilitary Ulster Volunteer Force. After his death the British Prime Minister, Tony Blair referred to Ervine's political journey: 'Though brought up in sectarian politics, he ended being a persistent and intelligent persuader for cross-community partnership and will be sorely missed'. David Adams, a journalist who knew Ervine well and was from a similar milieu,[4] contradicted Blair's assessment, pointing out that Ervine had not been brought up in sectarian politics, his father had been active in the labour movement and was a socialist:

> when he dedicated himself to helping end conflict and sectarian divisions it was, in essence, David Ervine's true nature manifesting itself. He was someone who came back to the socialism and non-sectarianism that he had learnt at his Father's knee.
>
> (*The Irish Times*, 13 January 2007)[5]

'A long way to get very little': the durability of ethno-national identity

How did the Irish Labour Party fair in the ethno-national cauldron of Northern Ireland? Very, very well is the surprising answer. But only for a short time. The northern section of the Irish Labour Party was mixed in composition, including members of the Socialist Republican Party, supporters of Jack Beattie and the ex-members of the NILP. Moreover the party was broadly based throughout Northern Ireland. In the 1949 local elections it won seven seats in Belfast and controlled the Warrenpoint and Newry Councils (Farrell 1980: 194). The party also had a strong presence in Derry. Macgougan described the party as an alliance of 'those who were labour with a national outlook and those who were nationalists with a slight working class bias' (Devine 1989: 119).

From this auspicious start, the Irish Labour Party seemed like it might make a breakthrough. In 1950 there was a breathtaking series of electoral battles for West Belfast in which Jack Beattie took on two notoriously sectarian unionist candidates one after the other before emerging triumphant by a margin of 25 votes (Macgougan was his agent on this occasion). Thereafter the alliance between nationally minded, anti-imperialist socialists and left nationalists began to fall apart in bitter in-fighting. The last remaining Irish Labour Party councillors in Belfast City Council lost their seats in 1958 and thereafter the party folded. Macgougan summed up his Irish Labour Party experience: 'I've come a long way to get very little' (Devine 1989: 120).

Michael Farrell presents the history of the northern section of the Irish Labour Party as one in a series of three occasions when the promise of working class unity was denied by sectarianism. The other occasions he mentions are the 1919 engineering strike in Belfast and 1932 'Outdoor Relief' crisis.

Perhaps in the failure of the labour movement to triumph over sectarianism, we can learn something about the durability of ethno-national identity?

Farrell's theory, which is the traditional Irish Marxist theory, is that sectarianism is an instrument of the state or the ruling class – familiar in the colonial context – to divide and rule the masses. It was precisely against this argument, with its naive economistic assumptions, that the young Paul Bew together with Peter Gibbon and Henry Patterson (1979) had invoked Louis Althusser: sectarianism had an autonomous existence within the working classes. The idea that it was an instrument to divide and rule was overly conspiratorial for neither the state nor the ruling class for the bourgeoisie 'operate according to the diktats of functional capitalist rationality' (O'Leary 2008). And yet, when one looks at the history of the 1919 and 1932 strikes and what happened after – both episodes of class unity were followed by fierce sectarian riots and ethnic cleansings – one can't simply dismiss Farrell's argument.

Thus, in the summer following the 1919 strike, up to 10,000 men and 1,000 women (Farrell 1980: 29) were put out of their workplaces by mobs led by the Ulster Unionist Labour Association. The Ulster Unionist Labour Association had been established in 1918 by the Ulster Unionist Council under the Chairmanship of Lord Carson. Most of the workers expelled were Catholics, but trade union activists and socialists were also targeted. 'Vigilance Committees' were established in the shipyards to, amongst other things, administer loyalty declarations on the part of workers seeking reinstatement. Henry Patterson describes the atmosphere in Belfast in the aftermath of the expulsions as 'intensely intolerant of any deviants' and notes that

> At the British TUC [Trade Union Congress] conference, a delegate from the National Association of Operative House and Ship Painters reported that, of 750 Belfast members, more than a hundred had refused to sign loyalty declarations and had been forced out, even though most had served during the war and more than twenty were Orangemen. At the Irish Labour Party and TUC one of the Belfast delegates maintained that more than four hundred protestant Labour supporters had been driven from the shipyards.
>
> (1980: 142)

Patterson comments that the goal of the Ulster Unionist Labour Association was not so much to secure a compliant workforce for Capital, but to secure ethnic unity as the national struggle in Ireland reached its climax.

The Outdoor Relief crisis presents a similar picture. In 1931 and 1932 an Outdoor Relief Workers Committee organised massive demonstrations of up to 60,000 Catholics and protestants against cuts in unemployment relief grants and their humiliating treatment at the hands of the Poor Law Guardians who dispensed them. The driving force behind the Committee was Tommy Geehan of the Revolutionary Workers Groups, helped by Betty Sinclair. Some of the demonstrations were broken-up by the police. Activists claimed that the subsequent riots were channelled into nationalist areas, and that only in these areas did police use their guns. Malachy Gray a member of the Revolutionary Workers Groups recalls

> during the . . . strike permission was given for the police to open fire in the nationalist areas. Two Catholics were shot dead by the police but no such action took place in unionist areas. It was an act of deliberate policy by the Government. From 1932 onwards there was continued sectarian incitement in the press and from political platforms.
>
> (1986: 111)

This time of fierce unemployment was when unionist politicians, including Prime Minster James Craig, made their most infamous calls for protestant employers to employ only protestants. The summer of 1935 saw another bout of communal rioting, workplace expulsions and ethnic cleansings during which labour premises were targeted.

My purpose in recounting this history is not to return us to the traditional Irish-Marxist argument that the persistence of ethnicity can be explained as a ruling class strategy of divide and rule. Rather it is to demonstrate, against the complacent consociational assertion that 'it was always thus', the extent to which the dominance of ethnopolitics in Northern Ireland was something that was worked at through a variety of practices and institutions.

Conclusion

'Though it appeared to be the antithesis of governance, "ethnic cleansing" is a technique of governmentality, a public-private partnership of violence that mixes professional military force and organisational logistics with freelance plunder, criminality and lawlessness'. So argue Gearóid Ó'Tuathail and Carl Dahlman (2004: 137) in relation to the strategy of the Milosevic regime in Bosnia. Likewise in the case of Northern Ireland: we should see the pogroms, workplace expulsions and riots that followed the episodes of cross-community activity in 1919, 1932 and 1968 as techniques of government.

Pogroms, and workplace expulsions have a spectacular quality and clearly repressive purpose, and were directed mainly at those identified as Catholics or nationalists. But we should note the evidence from 1920, that socialists and labour activists who were identified as protestants were also targeted. And with this in mind, we can perhaps begin to see pogroms and workplace expulsions as part of a continuum that included a variety of disciplinary techniques. Here the Foucauldian injunction to pay attention to the minor practices for governing people and their use by non-state as well as state institutions enables us to avoid some of the pitfalls of the traditional Marxist approach. For, as Valverde points out, Foucault's approach to power relations is surprisingly close to that of sociologists such as Erving Goffman who 'demonstrated that social power relations do not leap from structural economic relations, but are instead made and re-made every day in the encounters among individuals and groups that make up institutions' (2007: 160).

It is instructive in this context to return briefly to the break-up of the Northern Section of the Irish Labour Party in the 1950s. Here's how Farrell explains it:

> Under the pressure of Orange sectarianism they had been forced to confine themselves to the Catholic ghettos, only to be scattered and destroyed by the virulent anti-communism and anti-socialism of the Catholic Church in the 1950s and ghetto sectarianism against a mainly protestant-led party.
>
> (1980: 224)

Talk to almost any socialist active in the nationalist community in the 1930s, 1940s and 1950s and they speak of denunciations by the Catholic Church as one of the obstacles to their success. But this is well-known.

Jack Macgougan's experience can be used to illustrate the more subtle aspects of what Farrell is getting at. He recalled his experience as 'a youngster' helping his father campaign for Jack Beattie in East Belfast in the 1925 Stormont Election: 'we ran about with a red ribbon on and got into trouble with our classmates who were all unionists. That was the first time I was ever called a Fenian' (Devine 1989: 113; Macgougan may have been softening the language here: in this context the word 'Fenian' is a derogatory term for Catholic, but the vocabulary for betrayal and treachery in Northern Ireland is rich and colourful). Commenting on Macgougan's recollection, Devine quotes Hugh Minford, a unionist Minister in 1950 as saying: 'there are only two classes in Northern Ireland: the loyal and the disloyal. The loyal people are the Orangemen. The disloyal people are the socialists, communists and

Roman Catholics' (1989: 121). Such is the power of binary oppositions: if you are not with us you must be against us.

And yet even though Macgougan was frequently denounced as disloyal or as a 'Fenian' this did not necessarily lead to him being accepted as such by Catholics. As part of my research into the secession of the Derry Branch of the British-based union for which Macgougan was an organiser, I interviewed a retired shirt worker who, like most workers backed the breakaway union against Macgougan. She told me that for all his anti-partitionism, Macgougan was still regarded by the 'factory girls' as 'too British'. Such is the power of normative ethnicity.

Marilyn Hyndman who conducted a series of interviews with 'dissenting protestants' in the mid-1990s describes the difficulties some of her respondents experienced:

> still others discovered that free and open discussion within their own community was impossible and the cost of their silence, with its accompanying loneliness, was too high a price to pay. Ethnic cleansing is not just about burning and shooting people from their homes. It is also about the purging of dissenting voices.
>
> (1996: xvi)

When I read this quote, I thought again of Rosemary Harris, the anthropologist who was the first to conceive Northern Ireland as a plural society. If you look carefully, her discussion of the durability of group identity has an important twist to it. Harris agrees that for an individual to change group membership in the rural area of Northern Ireland that she studied would be very difficult psychologically and sociologically, 'at least while the individual remains in Northern Ireland'. But this is because of the 'strain' arising from communal sanctions and/or the 'the rupture in social ties presupposed by changed loyalties' (1986: 212), not because the individual's cultural identity and sense of self-worth would necessarily suffer damage. In this analysis communities are held together not so much by the warm embrace of primordial sentiment as by fear – whether of loneliness and/or communal sanction.

Such an analysis might alter one's perspective on the supposed virtues of cultural or segmental autonomy.

9 Conclusion

I set out to do three things in this book. The first was to construct a genealogy of a particularly influential approach to peace making, known as consociationalism. This approach has been the focus of a sustained 'liberal' critique, but has still managed to become the default approach of the liberal state when it comes to conflict resolution. 'Liberal' critics complain that consociation by recognising particular ethno-national identities in the name of equity or parity of esteem does not advance the cause of conflict resolution but institutionalises division and antagonism. Following on from that, my second aim was to answer a puzzle: how it was that the liberal state accommodated itself to apparently illiberal ethnic subjects and practices. I found an answer in anthropological ideas about culture and the plural society. Exploring the applications of these ideas in debates surrounding census data, anti-discrimination legislation, community relations work and so forth, it became apparent that what 'liberal' critics took as evidence of the 'failure' of consociation – for example, an apparent increase in communal segregation – was for the pioneer of consociation, an indicator of its success: make society more plural says Lijphart, recognise the ethnic protagonists and turn them into constructive elements of stable democracy. So, the 'liberal' critique of consociation misses the point, and that brings me to the third aim of this book; namely, to develop a more effective critique of the emerging common technology of peace.

Before getting into that, I would like to acknowledge the importance of the liberal critique of consociation and pause to consider its impact.

The impact of the liberal critique on policy post-conflict

There is clear evidence that the liberal critique of consociation has had a significant impact both at the level of the state and of the international community. Patrice McMahon and Jon Western conclude that the

Dayton peace agreement is a model to emulate because it ended the violence and built the conditions for a return to normal life for many. At the same time it offers a cautionary tale of the potential for institutional structures to create perverse incentives, spawn extremists, and undermine national unity.

(2009: 74)

It would appear that the joint proposals of the European Union and the United States regarding the future governance of Bosnia Herzegovina currently under discussion at camp Butmir have taken account of the Sejdic/Finci application to the European Court of Human Rights aimed at opening up the Presidency to ethnic minorities (International Crisis Group 12 November 2009).

In Northern Ireland, the emergence of the 'good relations' strategy articulated in *A Shared Future* (2005) and *Racial Equality* (2005) documents are a direct response by the British State to the old 'liberal' critique of consociation (Wilson 2009a). The *Shared Future* document bemoans communal segregation and ongoing conflict at communal interfaces. It states that 'Separate but equal is not an option. Parallel living and the provision of parallel services are unsustainable morally and economically' (OFMDFM 2005a: 15). The use of the phrase 'separate but equal' here is striking. In rejecting 'separate but equal', *A Shared Future* undoes the logic of parity of esteem elaborated by the Standing Advisory Commission on Human Rights (SACHR) 15 years before. If the reader recalls the discussion in Chapter 3, SACHR referred to the famous *Brown versus Board of Education* case (1954) which outlawed racial segregation in public education in the United States. In that case the Supreme Court ruled that separate but equal provision in public education could not provide African-Americans with the same standard of education as white Americans. Against this, SACHR attempted to salvage the notion of segregated education. It conceded that there were problems and added a few caveats, before concluding that such provision is 'an acceptable way of pursuing the objective of full equality of treatment and esteem' so long as the facilities are genuinely equal (1990: 79). SACHR claimed that a policy of equality of esteem would 'not necessarily result in an increase in . . . divisions and tensions' and, 'may also give leaders of the communities involved sufficient reassurance and confidence that their fundamental interests and values will not be ignored . . . to facilitate . . . the compromises necessary to achieve . . . joint participation in the structures of government' (1990: 87).

A Shared Future tackles head-on the debate between advocates of cross-community dialogue and advocates of single-identity work (see Chapter 5).

Without arbitrating, it insists that approaches to community relations 'that reinforce segregation must be challenged', and all forms of community relations work are subject to a test:

> all community development programmes should be required to identify how they will address sectarian and or racist behaviour to enable communities to work more effectively together and identify the expected good relations outcomes of their work. . . . In supporting any project, whether it is described as cross-community or single identity, the test is not the structure itself but the quality of the outcomes and whether they do in fact promote good relationship-building work.
>
> (OFMDFM 2005a: 41–42)

And yet with all that, this effort to promote what has become known as 'good relations' leaves the 'two community' approach intact: 'Community relations' refers specifically to division between the protestant and Catholic communities in Northern Ireland. 'Good Relations' refers to Section 75 of the Northern Ireland Act 1998 which includes 'persons of different religious belief, political opinion or racial group' (OFMDFM 2005a: 62).

The desire to go beyond the two communities model is to be welcomed, but as in the case of debates about human rights (see Chapter 7), one of the most striking outcomes of the *Shared Future* strategy is its novel variations on the ethnic norm. In the *Good Relations Indicators Baseline Report*, which will be used to monitor any change in good relations, there is a table itemising the changing composition of the Police Service of Northern Ireland, which makes a distinction between two categories: 'minority ethnic' and 'non-minority ethnic' (OFMDFM 2007: 117). Looking at the figures, it would appear that the 'non-minority ethnic' category is composed of members of the 'two communities'. Including a 'minority ethnic' category acknowledges that there are people in Northern Ireland beyond these 'two communities', but implies that what lies beyond is also ethnic.

One other feature of the liberal critique is that many of the critics are not liberals at all, but leftists who nevertheless end up endorsing individualism. For example Robin Wilson, who had a hand in drafting the *Shared Future* strategy, argues that it promotes a cosmopolitan notion of identity, which he, following David Held, defines as being 'based on three premises: Egalitarian individualism, which treats individuals not states or communities, as the unit of moral concern . . . Reciprocal recognition . . . Impartial treatment' (2009a: 99–100). Brian Graham and Catherine Nash agree that the *Shared Future* strategy articulates a form of individualism, but interpret it differently: not as evidence of cosmopolitanism but of an emerging neo-liberal agenda in post-conflict Northern Ireland: '*A Shared Future* embodies a bourgeois vision of a future society in Northern Ireland in which "deviant" sectarian division is replaced by the "normality" of economic individualism' (2006: 270).

Clearly the recourse to individualism even by leftist critics of consociation is problematic. We saw that in Bosnia Herzegovina, the critique of Dayton gave rise to a 'predictable debate' that revolved 'persistently around one or two poles: . . . on the one hand, the abstract citizen is insisted upon as the only genuine holder of rights, while on the other side, there [is the] absolutism and supreme authority of ethnic communities' (Hodžić 5 July 2006). Although writing mainly about post-conflict Serbia and Croatia, Stef Jansen's study of anti-nationalist discourse (2000) can be taken as further evidence of this phenomenon.

Jansen was disconcerted to find that for his respondents,

> the role and the importance of the self-interested and sovereign individual was sometimes privileged in almost evangelical terms. Also rationality and modernization, particularly through education, were high on the agenda for most of these who I would call established dissidents, and even in many of the more alternative critiques of nationalism.
>
> (2000: 227)

He was disconcerted by this because he had been hoping to find subaltern forms of solidarity and resistance. With this in mind, he notes that several of his respondents told him that had they lived in Western Europe, they would have been Greens or leftist,

> but given the situation in their own state, they felt they had to defend 'the individual' in ways that would be considered conservative in the 'West'. . . . the liberal discourse that was so dominant in anti-nationalism might have struck me as very mainstream, but they conceived it as a potential source of subversive material in an authoritarian and collectivist context.
>
> (Jansen 2000: 228)

He describes this as 'strategic individualism' and attempts to configure it for a radical politics. He quotes Slavoj Žižek (1992) and what Chen Xiaomei has described in the Chinese context as 'Occidentalism': 'it is an ethnocentric mistake of Western . . . "leftists" to exclude the possibility that some discourses that might support the status quo in one state hold subversive power in another' (Chen-Xiaomei 1996: 9)

In sum, the liberal critique of consociation and ethnopolitics has made an impact on post-conflict government in both Northern Ireland and the former Yugoslavia, but as basis for dissent it seems too easily absorbed and stymied or diverted into an individualism, the limits of which are familiar. Jansen quotes a dissident academic in Zagreb who had been vilified and lost his job because of his opposition to nationalism and doubted the feasibility of Jansen's study of anti-nationalism:

> it will be very hard . . . for you to find something in common between those people, apart from resistance to nationalism . . . we have very little, if anything, like a new collective identity. There are only individuals, like myself, who try to preserve their little microcosm and who would do anything not to end up in a new collective identity.
>
> (2000: 226)

At this point, the reader might be experiencing a feeling of *déjà vu*. One of the most familiar criticisms of Foucauldian analysis is that 'by insisting on the ubiquity and productivity of power, the possibility of resistance, transformation and the emergence of unforeseen possibilities is ruled out' (Armstrong 2008: 25). Taking into account my argument about the normativity of ethnicity in consociational agreements, and having just read the foregoing discussion of the limits of the liberal critique and the difficulties of resisting the priority given to ethno-nationalism in the GFA and Dayton Accords, the reader might suspect that my analysis is susceptible.

Genealogy and the problem of resistance

When developing an analysis one aspires to a certain clarity which can make the object of analysis appear more coherent than it is in reality. Certainly, I would not wish to give the impression that the peace agreements discussed in this book are characterised by a single dominant set of all-pervasive institutionalised norms. Far from it: to do so would be self-defeating for a book that is animated by an anxiety about the determinism of cultural essentialism and by a desire to broach the question of how those who are dubious about the call of the ethno-national might negotiate situations in which it is normative.

There are two inter-related issues that we must confront: one to do with conceptualising resistance, the other with analyzing institutions. With regard to the first, Brenner complains: 'all of the strategies of resistance Foucault mentions in his account of the "carceral system" are, in the last instance, rendered functional to the imperatives of disciplinary power' (1994: 700). With regard to the second, Marshall Sahlins argues that Foucault's monolithic view of power means that 'the actual substance of the institution' is reduced to 'its conjectured purposes and consequences'; that is, 'instrumental effects of discipline and control' (Sahlins 2002: 67). Although these issues are interrelated, I will deal with them separately, starting with the issue raised by Marshall Sahlins.

Of all Foucault's works, *Discipline and Punish*, is the one that veers closest to the functionalism of its era. There are two ways of responding to Sahlin's remarks. The first is to reiterate the point made in Chapter 5: key to the notion of governmentality that Foucault introduced in his lectures at the Collège de France is a methodology driven by the practices being studied and not by pre-existing concepts or 'generalized notions (such as "discipline") that have much heuristic utility but are inherently over simplifying' (Valverde 2008: 7). In other words, Foucault's later work was a response to, and dealt with, the criticisms of *Discipline and Punish*. But this is maybe to concede too much, because it might suggest that Foucault was a functionalist who repented late in life. This is not the case: the functionalism of *Discipline and Punish* should be seen as a lapse from Foucault's genealogical approach to intellectual history which, in line with its Nietzschean origins, was specifically anti-functionalist. This issue is worth exploring further because it can further illuminate the development of consociationalism in theory and in practice.

Dean, describes the genealogical approach to intellectual history as

> a way of linking historical contents into organized and ordered trajectories that are neither a simple unfolding of their origins nor the necessary realization of their ends. It is a way of analyzing multiple, open-ended, heterogeneous trajectories of discourses, practices, and events, and of establishing their patterned relationship, without recourse to regimes of truth that claim pseudo-naturalistic laws or global necessities.
>
> (Dean 1994: 35–36)

This emphasis on contingency is apt when looking at the development of consociationalism as a form of liberal governmentality. Foucault's conception of power/knowledge replaces sociological functionalism with a 'Nietzschean view of history as a play of "haphazard conflicts"' (Brenner 1994: 680). Governing practices and rationales are treated 'as being pragmatically put together, their success or failure being dependent on their usefulness not to "society" but rather to contenders in particular battles or struggles' (Valverde 2007: 161). Reading this quote, I was reminded of the consociationalist's response to the 'liberal' critique: a piece-meal and not entirely self-coherent elaboration of a distinction between 'corporate' and 'liberal' consociation.

I am also reminded of the development of the group designation procedures discussed in Chapter 4, especially the law introduced in the early 1990s to monitor the communal identity of job applicants and workforces. The power to ascribe to individuals a communal identity that they did not themselves choose is a good example of governmentality for it is devolved by the state to unnamed and unelected administrators in public and private organisations who are required to act according to a range of closely specified bureaucratic guidelines. At the time this was justified in terms of irreproachable aims. The purpose of the legislation was to correct a history of discrimination against Catholics as part of a universal idea of fairness that rejected all forms of discrimination: discrimination on religious grounds was singled out, but so too was gender. The bureaucratic recording of communal identity subsequently became a routine aspect of daily life in the 1990s: because of funding and evaluation requirements, various informal, civil society organisations began to compile and keep figures on the composition of members. And then it became central to the peace agreement signed in 1998, which requires elected members of the local legislature to designate a group identity. Later, in debates about a proposed Bill of Rights, these various group designation mechanisms and the associated procedures and rationales become the trump card for those arguing against the inclusion in the Bill of Rights of a right to determine one's own identity or even of exit from ethnic ascription. There is a pattern and an unimpeachable logic, but speaking as someone who played a bit-part in the implementation of anti-discrimination legislation in the early 1990s I can say that there was no inkling then that the normative ascription of ethnic identity was to be elevated to constitutional principle. Maybe I was short-sighted, but it seems to me that the pattern is only visible with hindsight: there is no teleology.

Towards a new critique

Writing in 2006, Richard Jenkins characterises Rogers Brubaker as arguing that ethnic groups do not exist and therefore should not be recognised. Jenkins suggests that for Brubaker, ethnicity is merely 'a point of view of individuals, a way of being in the world' (2006: 390), and identity is not real: 'it is not a "thing" that people can be said to have or to be' (2006: 391). Jenkins notes the relevance of Brubaker's work to the debates about human rights that we discussed in Chapters 3 and 7. In fact, as Jenkins notes, Brubaker visited Belfast in 2003 and participated in these debates. According to Jenkins, Brubaker regards the recognition of ethnic groups (granting them parity of esteem in the case of the GFA) as dangerous: 'the very instrument designed to promote equity and advance the cause of conflict resolution can, in fact, institutionalize ethnic divisions and antagonism' (2006: 392). He adds that Brubaker's views 'chime well with those of a range of Northern Irish commentators' (2006: 392); amongst those Jenkins mentions is the present author.

Whatever about Brubaker, it is not my view that identities and groups do not exist or that they should not be recognised (see Finlay 2004). My argument, and the argument of this book is that ethnic identity does not exist for everyone, all the time, in the same way. Contrary to those who believe that ethnicity is an essential quality that we all inherit, my argument is that ethnicity is not ubiquitous and that we should not take it for granted. Indeed, surely one of the key tasks of social science is precisely to examine the processes and circumstances in which identities and groups sometimes crystallise in forms that approximate to what essentialist theory might lead us to expect; that is as an emotionally laden, bounded, intense sense of belonging: a community of sentiment or affect (Aretxaga 2005).[1] The task is to study processes of crystallisation; that is, reification. Here I do agree with Brubaker, but for me the Foucauldian notion of subject formation and the role of power in that is the crucial thing.

As Nikolas Rose (1996) says subjection is a matter of government not of culture. To this I would add that cultural identity, ethnicity, is the regime of the person through which currently influential forms of governmentality work; certainly those like consociationalism and national multiculturalism that draw on a pluralist political rationale. Craig Calhoun sums up the regime of the person that underpins the normative power of ethnicity: 'two guiding assumptions in much modern thinking on matters of identity are that individuals ideally ought to achieve maximally integrated identities, and that to do so they need to inhabit self-consistent, unitary cultures or life-worlds' (1997: 18–19). Or, as Erik Erikson would have it: identity was 'a process located in the core of the individual and yet also in the core of his communal culture, a process which establishes . . . the identity of those identities' (1968: 22).

The productive power of the regime of the person through which consociational agreements work, is strengthened by the fact that it was originally articulated as a radical critique of, and resistance to, the ethnocentric assumptions and impositions of colonial powers (see Chapters 3 and 6). The response of the American Anthropological Association's Executive Board to the individualism of the Universal Declaration of Human Rights, drafted in 1947, states it succinctly:

The individual realizes his personality through his culture, hence a respect for individual differences entails a respect for cultural differences . . . There can be no individual freedom, that is, when the group with which the individual identifies is not free. There can be no full development of the individual personality as long as the individual is told, by men who have the power to enforce their commands, that the way of life of his group is inferior to that of those who wield the power.

(1947: 541)

Radical and critical as it once was, this view of identity is now part of a technology of government through which communities of resistance are brought in and made useful to government. But in the case of the GFA, what happened was not just the recognition of a northern nationalist identity that had been long oppressed, but the valorisation of the ethno-national as such. As we have argued in this book the problem with valorising ethnicity, incentivising it, making it normative, is that the space for other ways of being in the world and other forms of politics is reduced.

But this blanket valorisation of ethnicity is also expressive of another weakness of the GFA and it would appear of consociational forms more generally; that is an avoidance of 'the need for a societal narrative' dealing with past wrongs (Bell 2003: 1144): those committed during the conflict and those that gave rise to the conflict in the first place. In the absence of this it is difficult to criticise the normalisation of ethnicity because to do so might appear to undermine the gains in recognition and equality that have been made by the northern nationalist community. The question is: in these circumstances how do those for whom the 'call of the ethnic' is less than compelling, participate in public life?

Resisting ethnicity without undermining equality

As we saw in Chapter 4 the settled social scientific opinion would suggest that this is impossible: people born and socialised in Northern Ireland can be only one thing or the other: one is either a 'cultural catholic' or a 'cultural protestant' (e.g. see McGarry and O'Leary 1995: 502 and FitzGerald 1997). I have not found an answer to this dilemma in the broader literature on ethnicity or conflict resolution either. The places where it is broached include feminist political philosophy and postcolonial theory.

Even here, there are some who would suggest that the question is futile. Albert Memmi's influential book, *The Colonizer and the Colonized* (1990), attests to the power of colonial binaries, and the difficulty of escaping them. His portrait of the 'colonizer of goodwill' is based on a group of philosophy professors in Tunis. Memmi says he 'understood only too well their difficulties, their inevitable ambiguity and their resulting isolation; more serious still, their inability to act'. He understood them because 'all this was part of my own fate' (1990: 13). He explains how as a Tunisian Jew he was part of a group that was native, but which identified with the French and had privileges with respect to the Muslim population. The ambiguity and ambivalence that he describes is not so much to do with the difficulty of coming to terms with the violence of the struggle for national liberation: having debunked 'the myths of colonization', how 'could I complacently approve the counter-myths fabricated by the colonized?' (1990: 13). Hence the inability to act. Jean-Paul Sartre in the first introduction to the book elaborates on the theme of inaction-to-the-point-of-irrelevance of this stratum. Liam O'Dowd who writes the introduction to the second edition echoes this when he speaks of the shock of recognition when he read Memmi for the first time. Memmi spoke directly to the political ineffectiveness and personal dilemmas that he witnessed in the moderate humanists and leftists he met when he first came to teach at Queen's University Belfast in the mid 1970s when the conflict was at its height (1990: 38).

And yet some people did find within themselves the capacity to act. Not the rich and the upwardly mobile, as some might suggest, but ordinary working people such as the socialists whose careers we traced in Chapter 8. It has been suggested that socialists in Northern Ireland because they attempted to appeal to both communities were soft when it came to condemning discrimination against Catholics. This may be true of some, but it is not true of all. Take Jack Macgougan who appeared in the *Belfast Telegraph* styled as a 'Protestant Councillor' who now represented the Irish Labour Party on Belfast Corporation. He is quoted as saying:

> Those of us who are from the Unionist majority should examine our own conscience. Just as the ordinary German had to accept responsibility for the Nazi persecution of Jews and the American for the treatment of the coloured population . . . so we must accept responsibility for discrimination against the minority here.
>
> (Devine 1989: 123–24)

Firm in his anti-imperialism and his socialism, Macgougan was supple and loose in his ethnic identification, and a consistent critic of anti-Catholic discrimination (see also Macgougan 1948). But Macgougan's politics are of their time: where today can those for whom the 'call of the ethnic' is less than compelling find the practical, political and theoretical resources to intervene in public life?

Dis-identification

The work of feminist theorists, particularly Judith Butler, provides one resource. This is in itself salutary: here are people willing to tackle the taken-for-grantedness of sex, which appears to be a much more 'natural' and fundamental part of our identities than ethnicity! Here is what Butler says:

> the category of 'sex' is, from the start, normative; it is what Foucault has called a 'regulatory ideal'. In this sense . . . 'sex' not only functions as a norm, but is part of a regulatory practice that produces the bodies it governs, that is whose regulatory force is made clear as a kind of productive power, the power to produce – demarcate, circulate, differentiate – the bodies it controls.
>
> (1993: 1)

If the problem is 'the tendency of normalizing disciplinary power to tie individuals to their identities in constraining ways, and thus sustain relations of domination' (Armstrong 2008: 24), we can agree with Foucault that the task 'is not to discover what we are, but to refuse what we are' (Afterword to Dreyfus and Rabinow 1982: 216). Resistance involves dis-identification.

This goes back to Louis Althusser, or rather the response of Michel Pecheux, the French linguist, to Althusser's work on subject formation. Confronted by normalising power, one could be a 'good subject' or a 'bad subject'. A good subject is one who identifies with, and assimilates to, the norm and suffers the consequences. There were two kinds of 'bad subject'. One kind of bad subject counter-identified: inverting the dominant symbolic system such that a stigmatised characteristic or identity is rendered positive.

The problem with counter-identification is that it leaves the dominant symbolic system intact, validating it through what Esteban Munoz calls a controlled symmetry of 'counterdetermination' (1999: 11). Worse, as Aurelia Armstrong argues, those who are oppressed by power can come to be invested in that oppression 'in so far as their self-identity becomes bound up with the terms through which they are marginalized, excluded and discriminated against. In other words, politicized identity becomes attached to its exclusion because its existence is premised on this exclusion' (2008: 23). Many have noted the intimacy which often binds the adversaries in a civil war together 'with each one depending on the other for its own definition and legitimacy' (Aretxaga 2005: 173). The palpable discomfit of Unionist politicians when the IRA first declared a ceasefire is one example. But so too may be the attachment of some nationalist politicians to mechanisms of group designation in employment legislation and the local assembly.[2]

The other kind of bad subject is one who dis-identifies. One can find some references to dis-identification in the literature on Northern Ireland and the former Yugoslavia, though it is rarely described as such. Whitaker (2004) is an exception. During her research on the Northern Ireland Women's Coalition, she met various individuals who explicitly dissented from the available identity categories, mostly the protestant/unionist/British category (see also Hyndman 1996). In the case of the former Yugoslavia, Jansen quotes Peki, 'an elderly refugee', who 'said he had enough of having to declare himself on official and unofficial forms . . . he didn't know anymore to which category he belonged: was he in Serbia, or in Republika Srpska, or in Bosnia, or in Yugoslavia?' (2000: 89). Jansen then quotes a writer, Slavko, who says

> we all worked on being citizens [of the former Yugoslavia] and now there are only Croats and Serbs and so on. At the census a lot of people declared as Eskimos or as Chinese, really a lot. They don't accept it . . . I wrote 'Jew'. It was my way to escape . . . it doesn't mean much either.
>
> (2000: 89)

These examples of dis-identification seem highly individualised and we should note that Slavoj Žižek has disputed the subversive potential of dis-identification. Instead of dis-identification, Žižek suggests a strategy of over-identification: 'simply taking the power discourse at its (public) word, acting as if it really means what it explicitly says (and promises) – can be the most effective way of disturbing its smooth functioning' (2000a: 220; see also 2000b). I agree that counter-identification can be a potent strategy,[3] but I do not want to give up on dis-identification just yet.

Here is how Judith Butler describes dis-identification:

> if my options are loathsome, if I have no desire to be recognized within a certain set of norms, then it follows that my sense of survival depends upon escaping the clutch of those norms by which recognition is conferred. It may well be that my sense of social belonging is impaired by

the distance I take, but surely that estrangement is preferable to gaining a sense of intelligibility by virtue of norms that will only do me in from another direction. Indeed, the capacity to develop a critical relation to these norms presupposes a distance from them, an ability to suspend or defer the need for them, even as there is a desire for norms that might let one live. The critical relation depends as well on a capacity, *invariably collective*, to articulate an alternative, minority version of sustaining norms or ideals that enable me to act.

(2006: 3, my emphasis)

There are two things about this quote that seem important, and that I wish to focus on as I bring this book to a conclusion. The first is Butler's caution; the second is her emphasis on the idea that to be effective dis-identification needs to be collective. I would like to consider each of these issues in turn.

Butler's caution is rooted in her appreciation that while norms and regulatory ideals can 'do you in', they are also productive. A regulatory ideal such as sex produces the bodies it governs. It is productive also in the sense that we all need the kind of recognition that subjection confers: it is only 'through the experience of recognition that any of us becomes constituted as socially viable beings' (2006: 2). It is only through identification and subjection that life becomes liveable. But that only makes the predicament worse: 'without some recognizability I cannot live . . . [but] these terms by which I am recognized make life unliveable' (2006: 4). This is the predicament of those who are misrecognised by a powerful external agent and ascribed an identity that does not fit.

Butler discusses the practical implications of this analysis for how one might respond in situations where there are competing and contradictory identity claims. Her discussion focuses on a particular conundrum in the field of sexual politics. On the one hand there is 'queer theory's claim to be opposed to the unwanted legislation of identity' or categorisation. Against this is the transsexual's apparent desire to become a man or a woman: a desire that is to conform to an established identity category, even if that means elective surgery.[4] And then there is an intersex movement that defends the integrity of intersexed conditions against compulsory reassignment surgery. Having explored the tensions between these different positions, Butler concludes:

the task of all of these movements seems to me to be about distinguishing among the norms and conventions that permit people to breathe, to desire, to love, and to live and those norms and conventions that restrict or eviscerate the conditions of life itself. Sometimes norms function both ways at once, and sometimes they function one way for a given group, and another way for another group. What is important is to stop legislating for all lives what is liveable only for some, and similarly, to refrain from proscribing for all lives what is unliveable for some.

(Butler 2004: 8)

It seems to me that this conclusion might be of broader relevance: alerting us to the dangers of legislating for identity, suggesting that we think carefully about whether it is absolutely necessary.

The second point about dis-identification that I wish to pick up on is Butler's insistence that to be viable it needs to be collective. Whitaker documents the complex and contradictory and unsettled identities of some of the women she met while doing her research with the Northern Ireland Women's Coalition. On the basis of this, and of her analysis of the re-designation controversy in the legislature established by the GFA, Whitaker concludes that what might be important is not differences between groups, nor even differences within groups, but difference within individual subjects. For feminists like Judith Butler, Donna Haraway and Robin Whitaker it is not the whole, integrated subject privileged by Erik Erikson and cultural pluralism that is valorised, but the fractured and conflicted subject. But the point is that Whitaker's fractured subjects did not remain alone with their internal conflicts: they made a home – or temporary shelter at least – in the Northern Ireland Women's Coalition.

It is possible to create such spaces. Spaces where what Leela Gandhi (2006: 185) has called a 'dissident relationality' might flourish. The context for Gandhi's exploration of dissident relationality is the '"minor" politics' that underpinned anti-imperialist and cross-cultural solidarity in Britain at the end of the nineteenth century. The minor politics she refers to included libertarian socialism, sexual reform, animal rights and spiritualism: a late Victorian counter-culture that coalesced around the figure of Edward Carpenter. These are things that serious socialists hated: at that time Engels referred to them as a hopeless 'mishmash' and Lenin later denounced them as an 'infantile disorder' (Gandhi, 2006: 12). George Orwell was still complaining about 'sandal-wearers' when he wrote *The Road To Wigan Pier* in 1937. Gandhi's is only one of several re-evaluations of the significance of this late-Victorian counter-culture (see Rowbotham 2009)

Which is to return us to the theme with which we started; namely, the unappreciated potential of the counter-cultural as a facilitator of the inter-cultural in conflict and post-conflict societies. This is not just 'punk nostalgia' (McLoone 2004) or the idealism of a deracinated academic, but the practical advice of a seasoned community relations worker in Bosnia, who believes strongly in the potential of cultural programmes, but not those in which, singly or together, the folk cultures and ethnic identities of the participants are raised to the highest virtue. This is just 'a reproduction/reinforcement of differences'. Rather the kind of programmes he wants to experiment with are those that draw on '"alternative" (underground, countercultural, OFF, call it as you like) cultural paradigms, which offer . . . additional points of identification, potential (not necessary) transcendence of ethnic identity'.

Notes

1 Introduction

1 The Good Friday Agreement is named after the day that it was signed (10 April 1998), with all of the implied symbolism. For that very reason some prefer to call it after the place were it was signed: the Belfast Agreement. I have used 'Good Friday Agreement' because it appears to be the more frequent in common usage. For example if you enter 'Good Friday Agreement' into Google there are 39,800,000 results as against 326,000 for 'Belfast Agreement'.

2 In addition to documentary research relating to the GFA and the Dayton Accords, I made three study-visits to the Balkans: in May and September 2007 to Bosnia-Herzegovina and September 2008 to Slovenia and Bosnia-Herzegovina. I also draw on ongoing correspondence with colleagues in Bosnia. Where possible I have tried to preserve the anonymity of the various people I have met with, avoiding real names when I could and occasionally disguising locations and events. The book draws on various pieces of research conducted in Northern Ireland over many years; the nature of this research is discussed at relevant points in the text.

3 Jenny Edkins (2006) interprets the hidden purpose of prisons as being the depoliticisation of an underclass of people and by extension draws attention to the importance of subjugated knowledges in the genealogy of conflict. I am grateful to Mick O'Broin for drawing my attention to Edkin's article and its relevance to my own argument (see O'Broin 2008).

2 Anthropology, cultural pluralism and consociational theory

1 In Lijphart's subsequent work M. G. Smith disappears altogether. The honour of 'discovering' consociation is attributed to another scholar of West Africa, Sir Arthur Lewis (Lijphart 1995).

2 Harris supervised my PhD thesis, but I don't think that I am exaggerating her significance here. Anthony Buckley (2008: 169) says Harris's book 'transformed ethnology' in Northern Ireland. McGarry and O'Leary invoke her as someone who agrees that 'Northern Ireland is a segmented society with a clear social boundary between two major communities' and describe her ethnography as 'exemplary' (1995: 185 and 446).

3 Paddy Ashdown, the former High Representative of the International Community to Bosnia-Herzegovina (2002–6) and Chair of the Strategic Review of Parading in Northern Ireland (2007–?), defended the institutionalisation of ethnicity by the GFA and the Dayton Accords by arguing that the enmities of civil war take a very long time to heal (personal communication, 6 December 2006). By way of illustration, Ashdown mentioned that the bitterness of the English Civil war took several hundred years to heal.

3 Essentialism and the reconciliation of the liberal state to ethnicity

1 Anthropologists have been struggling for years to account for the apparent durability of ethnicity without reifying ethnic groups. One of the most influential attempts was by Frederik Barth (1969). Ethnic identities are not primordial, they are constructed and maintained by people in interaction. Barth drew particular attention to interaction at the boundary: it is the construction of external difference that generates internal sameness or similarity. Ultimately Barth does not quite escape the old anthropological idea of culture: the boundary metaphor is suggestive of a relativistic view of the world as a mosaic of groups each with their own culture and values (Jenkins 1996). Like all symbolic interactionist theories, Barth's is susceptible to the criticism that it neglects power relations.

2 Commenting on the American intervention in the Middle East, a number of scholars have noted the apparent centrality to military strategy of the 'old' idea of culture. In this context, the old idea of culture suggests that 'different ways of life produce different ways of war' (Porter 2007: 45). Thus, according to the clash of civilisations rhetoric, the war on terror is portrayed as being between secular, liberal, universalistic American-led forces on one side, and Jihadist warriors and tribal warlords on the other. In line with the rhetoric, the United States military has been sponsoring social research and recruiting social scientists, particularly anthropologists, to provide cultural awareness training to its troops. Following the old idea of culture, the logic is that to wage war effectively one must know one's enemy and to do that one must know their culture. For the United States military in Baghdad, 'firepower seems to have become "less important than learning to read the signs"'. In February 2006 a new American Army Field manual was released which outlines what Derek Gregory calls 'hermeneutics of counterinsurgency'. The manual states 'American ideas of what is "normal" or "rational" are not universal. To the contrary, members of other societies often have different notions of rationality, appropriate behaviour . . . norms concerning gender'. For this reason, it was necessary 'to avoid imposing' American ideas of the normal and the rational on other people (Gregory 2008: 8). The cultural turn in military strategy is sometimes presented as a liberal and progressive move such that anthropologists are regarded as potential allies for supposedly 'more progressive forces within the pentagon who would like to develop a more multilateral, culturally informed set of foreign policies and military practices' (Lutz 2008: 1). Nevertheless, these developments have provoked a fierce response from social scientists, particularly anthropologists, about the ethics of military sponsorship of social science research (Gonzalez 2007, 2008 and 2009; Kilcullen 2007; McFate 2007; Price 2007 and 2008; Lutz 2008; Robben 2009). One would hope that these developments might also provoke some reflection on the changing nature of war, counterinsurgency and pacification.

4 Is ethnopolitics a form of biopolitics?

1 The republican movement led a successful campaign to boycott the 1981 census during which one census collector was shot dead.
2 The Statistical and Social Inquiry Society of Ireland was formed in 1847 in the tradition of British colonial administration. It is the oldest social science body in Ireland.
3 The oddness of McCrudden's appeal to the phenomenon of 'telling' is perhaps best captured by Kevin Rooney when he describes his experience as a young man growing up at what would now be called a interface between Catholic and protestant communities. 'It was always a good idea to know every word of either the Hail Mary or the Sash in case you were challenged as to your religion.' Knowing the Hail Mary covered you if the people who challenged you were Catholic; knowing the Sash (an orange song) if they were protestant. Being found out of place resulted in a beating or worse. Rooney comments:

> Twenty years on this kind of backward sectarian division is now being celebrated on all sides. They may not be reciting the Rosary or singing the Sash, but by standing up in the new Assembly and designating themselves as part of one tradition or the other, they may as well be. Some breakthrough!
>
> (Rooney 1998: 21)

4 This research involved participant observation at trade union conferences and meetings and weekend workshops attended by shop stewards, facilitated by community relations experts. There was some formal and informal interviewing, and evaluation surveys were conducted at the end of each of the workshops (see McWilliams and Finlay 1992 and Finlay 1992, 1993 and 1998).

5 Consociationalism as a form of liberal governmentality: 'single-identity work' versus community relations

1 The first Community Relations Council was wound up by the short-lived power-sharing assembly established following the Sunningdale Agreement in 1974.
2 One can detect Church *et al.*'s (2004) own ambivalence. And on occasion officers of the Community Relations Commission have insisted that

> all local cultures are 'eligible' to work with the Cultural Diversity Programme . . . [and] whatever influence we have seeks to encourage mutual acknowledgement . . . CRC . . . support . . . is based upon a project's potential for improved community relations, not any desire for cultural affirmation. Groups with relatively fixed ideological positions are very welcome to engage with us, but they are unlikely to gain more than advice unless they are prepared to open a meaningful dialogue with others or critically reflect on their own history.
>
> (Langlois 2000: 18)

This came as part of the response to a critique of the promotion of Ulster-Scots culture (see also Nash 2005).
3 Rolston (1980) notes that the first Community Development Officer appointed in 1970 had previously worked in community development in Zambia.

4 As its first Development Officer says, the Cultural Traditions Group 'came together' at a conference held in 1989, 'Came together' is apt and aptly Foucauldian – the organisation was not announced by government but crystallised at an invited conference of people prominent in local cultural life. Also aptly Foucauldian is the description of this work as 'pre-political' (see Finlay 2004). Only with hindsight does it become apparent that it was part of a larger initiative under the sponsorship of the new Community Relations Agency provided for in the Anglo-Irish Agreement and prefigured by Frazer and Fitzduff (1994).

5 Amongst community relations practitioners themselves, one can find a similar practical wisdom regarding the limitations of cross-community or 'trans-ethnic' work. One Bosnian community relations worker told me:

> There is a tendency in BiH [Bosnia-Herzegovina] society, in everyday life, I think again due to its heterogeneity, to avoid situations that might disturb social order, to avoid conflicting, to cool down, etc . . . It includes not only relations among people, there is also avoidance of unknown (social/cultural) practices, everything that might change 'regular relationship' among people. There is a proverb (actually used in all Yugoslavia) which says: 'Peaceful Bosnia!' (Mirna Bosna!). One usually uses it when successfully finish some work on mutual benefit: 'I've done it, peaceful Bosnia'. It is kind of reciprocity that you should take care when doing something, otherwise 'Bosnia' is not peaceful, and everybody lose. If you behave different . . . social order . . . is potentially jeopardized.
>
> (personal communication 12 December 2009)

'Mirna Bosna' made me think of a saying sometimes used in Northern Ireland: 'whatever you say, say nothing'. Seamus Heaney uses this saying as the title of one of his best-known poems, published in 1975. 'Whatever you say, say nothing' refers to a profound reticence and politeness in social encounters with members of the other ethnic community. This reticence/politeness, as sequel to 'telling', is a way of managing the alienation of a divided society, and it is so powerful that it was possible for some to imagine that social relations in Northern Ireland were basically good (Donnan and McFarlane 1983). The consequence is that genuine dialogue about any serious matters is very difficult, fraught or even impossible (see Burton 1978, and Finlay 1999), with obvious implications for inter-cultural dialogue and community relations work.

6 The single-identity approach to community relations is also used in Israel/Palestine where it is called 'uninational' work (see Church *et al.* 2004).

6 Paradigm shifts and the production of 'national being'

1 Phillip Gleason (1983) is very good on the semantic history of the term 'identity' in the United States of America. He notes that the *Encyclopedia of the Social Sciences* first published in the early 1930s carries no entry for 'identity' and that the *International Encyclopedia of the Social Sciences*, 1968, carries only two substantial articles, one on psychosocial identity, another on political identification. The dictionary of sociology I bought while a student in the 1980s contains no entry for the term identity (Abercrombie *et al.* 1984, 1988 2nd edition).

2 That loyalists got the message is evidenced by the sudden appearance in 1992 of the slogan: 'Our Message to the Irish is simple: hands off Ulster, Irish Out. The

Ulster conflict is about nationality'. The slogan was initially painted at Freedom Corner on the Newtownards road in Belfast as part of a mural with Cúchulainn as its centre-piece (Bill Rolston, personal communication 7 April 2009). In Irish mythology Cúchulainn is the champion of Ulster. The mural described him as 'ancient defender of Ulster from Irish attacks over 2000 years'. This association might make the nation alluded to in the slogan ambiguous: is it some putative Ulster nation or the British nation? In any case, the mural has been repainted several times and it is perhaps significant that Cúchulainn is no longer the centre piece.

3 O'Halloran writes that one of the most potent stereotypes of northern protestants in the Republic of Ireland was that of the 'hard-headed unionist', rational, adept in business and economic matters. However, she notes that this positive stereotype could tip over into a view of Unionists as 'cynical, amoral materialists' lacking in 'idealism' and culture (1987: 46–47).

4 A popular narrative of deracination is articulated by Billy Mitchell in an interview with Susan McKay. Mitchell was a loyalist ex-prisoner who worked in 'conflict transformation' after his release. He explained one of the problems facing working-class protestant communities:

> The trouble is on our side, whenever someone gets on, becomes a lawyer or a journalist, they forsake their roots. Once they get a wee bit respectable, they don't want to be reminded that they came from among the riff raff in Tiger's Bay or Mount Vernon. They go off to north Down and distance themselves. On the other side, in the Nationalist community, there is more solidarity. Their professional people haven't left them. They give something back.
>
> (McKay 2000: 60–61)

In addition to the political abdication of the bourgeoisie, Mitchell probably also has in mind the hypocrisy of those who condemn bigotry from a safe distance.

5 With this in mind, we should recall the intellectual roots of consociational theory in writing about, and from, the colonial and postcolonial world – for example, M. G. Smith's work – and the conviction of leading consociationalists of the relevance of the colonial frame for Ireland. McGarry and O'Leary's emphasis on colonialism as a frame for Ireland makes their apparent disavowal of culture all the more curious (e.g. see 2009: 367 and 383). For it is the 'cultural turn' that has breathed new life into colonial studies. Thomas sums up the key idea:

> colonialism is not best understood primarily as a political or economic relationship that is legitimized . . . through ideologies of racism or progress. Rather, colonialism has always, equally importantly and deeply, been a cultural process . . . Colonial cultures are not simply ideologies that mask, mystify or rationalize forms of oppression that are external to them; they are . . . constitutive of colonial relationships themselves.
>
> (Thomas 1998: 2)

7 No exit: human rights and the priority of ethnicity

1 In 2006, the Women's Coalition celebrated its tenth anniversary by winding up its affairs. According to Barbara McCabe, it is not the case that the Women's Coalition lost out 'in the rush for the extremes' following the signing of the GFA. But she does elaborate a contrast between the political conditions prevailing when the Women's

Coalition was formed and the conditions when it collapsed. The broadly based peace talks that preceded the GFA 'challenged the majoritarian view of politics' and opened up a space for the Coalition, but once 'majoritarianism took root again, the space for creative problem-solving gave way to horse trading – and when the only thing that matters is the size of your horse, it doesn't matter how novel your contribution might have been' (McCabe 2006: 7).

2 The St Andrews Agreement of October 2006 resulted in the restoration of the Northern Ireland Assembly. The agreement was reached after negotiations involving the British and Irish Governments and the main local political parties, especially the Democratic Unionist Party and Sinn Fein.

3 The original idea, provided for in the GFA, was for a newly formed Northern Ireland Human Rights Commission to liaise with a new Irish Human Rights Commission to draft a joint charter of rights for the island as a whole. Aside from the difficulties experienced in the north, the work of the Irish Human Rights Commission was adversely affected by cuts to its budget in 2009.

4 Whitaker (2010) does not have a problem with the fact that human rights processes give rise to political conflict, but that the emphasis on rights can direct the scope of political conflict in limiting ways: political action become a matter of pursuing rights and courts become the focus of the action, which requires resource in terms of money and expertise.

5 There is a difference between the two processes that McCrudden elides. The designation rules for members of the local legislature have an opt-out, albeit with diminished status. Employment monitoring procedures do not allow people socialised locally to opt-out of the two categories, assigning them to one or other category against their will if necessary.

6 The Standing Advisory Commission on Human Rights recognised the work of the Community Relations Council in promoting cultural traditions, but argued that constitutional recognition of the 'two main sections of the community' was needed because without it there was no guarantee that 'objectionable measures might not be enacted in the future'. The focus of its concern was the nationalist minority, but it argued that,

> similar considerations apply in respect of the protection of the unionist and British tradition in parts of Northern Ireland where nationalists are in control or more generally if the government of Northern Ireland were to be controlled by parties more interested in or committed to the nationalist or Irish tradition.
>
> (1990: 90)

7 It is also worth noting that the NIHRC did not take up a suggestion from the 'Women's sector' of the Human Rights Forum to mention 'sexual orientation minorities' in the 'Identity and Culture' section.

8 This cultural racism draws on the same pluralist political rationality that underpins the GFA and liberal multiculturalism more generally. Thus migrants are attacked not because they are biologically inferior but because they are a threat to 'our way of life'. The appropriation of the language of multiculturalism by racists is not peculiar to Northern Ireland (see Wright 1998), but it has a specific resonance in the context of the peace process. And so, the excuse given for the intimidation of Chinese people living and working in a part of South Belfast was that they posed a

threat to the heritage, way of life and Britishness of local protestant residents (see Finlay 2004 and 2006).

8 'A long way to get very little': the durability of identity, socialist politics and communal discipline

1 I am grateful to Dick Hunter for providing me with a copy of this interview transcript. I myself interviewed Macgougan on several occasions, including at his home in Milton Keynes on 8 June 1983 and 24 March 1987. The interviews focussed less on his political work than on his experience as Irish Organiser for the National Tailor and Garment Workers Union (NUTGWU), a position which he held from 1945 to 1968 when he was elected General Secretary of the NUTGWU. (Macgougan thought twice before taking up this post because it required him to leave Northern Ireland just as the Troubles broke out.) This research was conducted as part of larger project on trade unionism and sectarianism in the Derry Shirt industry 1921–68, based on documentary research and life-history interviews (see Finlay 1989).

2 This view of identity change as conversion might be compared with common sense views of identity change as betrayal. There is a rich language for betrayal in Ireland. Among nationalists there is: Castle-Catholic, Shoneen, West-Brit. These are variations on the theme of subservience or assimilation to Britain or the British administration in Ireland. Among unionists there is: Lundy, Fenian-lover, or guilty-prod sometimes fore-shortened to 'guilty'. Lundy was Governor of Londonderry who tried to surrender the city to a besieging Catholic army in 1689. Fenian is a protestant term of abuse for Catholic, and Fenian-lover self-explanatory. 'Guilty-Prod' is someone who is ashamed of his or her roots and is excessively conciliatory to Irish nationalism. This is the oppressive binary logic – if you are not with us you are against us – that we know from writing about the colonial world (see Aretxaga 1997), and gender (Butler 2006: 2).

3 This is an article put together by Francis Devine based on interviews carried out by Francis Devine and Dick Hunter.

4 Adams was a member of the Ulster Democratic Party, a party with links to the loyalist Ulster Defence association and stood as a candidate in the first Assembly election.

5 Macgougan and Ervine are very different in character and in politics. The one austere and disciplined, the other easygoing and jokey. But it may not be too far-fetched to suggest that they shared a capacity to play fast and loose with their supposed protestant and Unionist 'roots' for rhetorical and performative effect. Francis Devine was shown a newspaper clipping in Macgougan's papers. The source and precise date were not noted, but it was clearly from the *Belfast Telegraph* in 1956. It is worth quoting for two reasons. First, for what it tells us about identity. Second, because it gives the lie to those who would argue the labour movement failed to take a stand against anti-Catholic discrimination.

The clipping styles Macgougan as a 'Protestant Councillor' representing the Irish Labour Party on Belfast Corporation, and quotes him as saying

> Those of us who are from the Unionist majority should examine our own conscience. Just as the ordinary German had to accept responsibility for the Nazi persecution of Jews and the American for the treatment of the coloured

population . . . so we must accept responsibility for discrimination against the minority here.

(Devine 1989: 123–24)

Macgougan was a frequent critic of discrimination (see also Macgougan 1948).

9 Conclusion

1 One problem with Brubaker is his emphasis on identification and categorisation as purely cognitive processes with no affective bases or consequences (see Brubaker and Cooper 2000).

2 The tentative willingness of Mark Durkhan, former leader of the Social Democratic and Labour Party, to contemplate a future in which the 'ugly scaffolding' of group designation in the local legislature could be deconstructed is particularly notable here (*Hearts and Minds*, BBC2 Northern Ireland 19 September 2009).

3 Examples of over-identification with an explicit discourse of power are hard to find. The most familiar (because articulated by Žižek himself) is Laibach, the music wing of Slovenian art collective NSK (Neue Sloweische Kunst). Laibach was the German name for the Slovenian capital city during the Nazi occupation. Amongst other musical styles Laibach project is a strident volkish brand of metal music.

Another, much more fraught example of over-identification might be the campaign by republican prisoners to achieve Special Category or political status. The hunger strike in which ten prisoners died was the culmination of this campaign, but it was preceded by a 'dirty protest'. The dirty protest had its origins in the prisoners' refusal to wear prison uniform. This refusal prompted a retaliation by the prison authorities and the protest escalated until 1978 when prisoners refused to leave their cells except to go to Mass and visits. Unable to empty chamber pots, the prisoners began to smear faeces on the walls of their cells. As Aretxaga (2004 and 2005; see also Feldman 1991) points out the dirty protest had no precedent in the political culture and was met with incomprehension by the prison authorities and the government and the British general public. To understand it, it needs to be located in the colonial stereotypes discussed in Chapter 6. As Aretxaga points out:

Dirtiness has been a metaphor of Barbarism in British anti-Irish discourse for centuries . . . thus I would argue that the fantasies of savagery projected onto Catholics were appropriated, literalized, and enacted by the prisoners. This materialization inevitably confronted the officers in an inescapable form with their own fantasies, which produced shock, horror, and the futile attempt to erase them by increasing violence, forced baths, and periodic steam cleaning of cells – acts of cleansing that, like the dirtying of the prisoners, were both literal and symbolic. The 'Dirty Irish' had become really shitty . . . exposing . . . a scathing critique of Britain and, by association, of civilisation.

(2005: 66–67)

4 As Kate Bornstein points out it may not be a desire to conform to an established identity category, but simply the desire for transformation itself (Butler 2006: 8).

Bibliography

Abazović, D. (2007) 'Introduction: reflections on the presence of the international community in the BiH society', in *Proceedings From The Conference Examples of Bosnia and Herzegovina: sustainable concepts or lost ways of the international community*, Sarajevo: Heinrich Boll Foundation and Office for Bosnia and Herzegovina.

Abercrombie, N., Hill, S. and Turner, B. S. (1984, 1988 second edition) *The Penguin Dictionary of Sociology*, London: Penguin Books.

Adams, D. (13 January 2007) 'A Peacemaker at the Start and the Finish', *The Irish Times*.

Agamben, G. (2005) *State of Exception*, Chicago: University of Chicago Press.

Ahern, B. (2000) in P. Logue (ed.) *Being Irish: personal reflections on Irish identity today*, Dublin: Oak Tree Press.

Alliance Party of Northern Ireland (2001) *Response to the Northern Ireland Human Rights Commission's Draft Bill of Rights*, November 2001, Submission 124, Belfast: NIHRC. Available: http://billofrights.nihrc.org/submissions/submission_124.pdf (accessed 27 October 2009).

——(31 March 2008) 'Press Release: alliance comments on Bill of Rights Forum report release'. Available: http://www.allianceparty.org/news/ 003681/ alliance_comments _on _bill_of_rights_forum_report_release.html (accessed 15 May 2009).

Allport, G. (1954) *The Nature of Prejudice*, Reading, Mass.: Addison-Wesley.

Althusser, L. (1971) 'Ideology and Ideological State Apparatuses', in L. Althusser (ed.) *Lenin and Philosophy and Other Essays*, New York: Monthly Review Press.

Amalgamated Transport and General Workers Union (1993*) Equality for All: winning equality at work, an ATGWU guide*, Belfast: ATGWU.

Anderson, J. (2006) 'Undoing Territorial "Solutions": partition, consociation, integration and border-crossing democracy', 7th Mediterranean Social and Political Research Meeting, Robert Schuman Centre for Advanced Studies, European University Institute Florence, 22–26 March 2006.

Anderson, J. and Shuttleworth, I. (1994) 'Sectarian Readings of Sectarianism: interpreting the Northern Ireland census', *The Irish Review*, 16: 74–93.

Aretxaga, B. (1997) *Shattering Silence: women, nationalism and political subjectivity in Northern Ireland*, New Jersey: Princeton University Press.

—— (2004) 'Dirty Protest: symbolic overdetermination and gender in Northern Ireland', in N. Scheper-Hughes and P. Bourgois (eds) (2004) *Violence in War and Peace*, Oxford: Blackwell.

—— (2005) *States of Terror: Begona Aretxaga's essays*, Centre for Basque Studies Occasional Paper Series 10, Reno: University of Nevada.

Armstrong, A. (2008) 'Beyond Resistance: a response to Žižek's critique of Foucault's subject of freedom', *Parrhesia*, 5: 19–31.

Aughey, A. (2007, 1997) 'A State of Exception: the concept of the political in Northern Ireland', in C. McGrath and E. O'Malley (eds) *The Irish Political Studies Reader*, London and New York: Routledge.

Badiou, A. (2007) *Being and Event*, London: Continuum.

Balakrishnan, G. (2002) 'The Age of Identity' (Review of Lutz Niethammer, *Kollektive Identitat. Heimliche Quellen einer unheimlichen Konjunktur*, Hamburg: Reinback bei), *New Left Review,* 16: 130–42.

Barth, F. (ed.) (1969) *Ethnic Groups and Boundaries: the social organization of culture difference*, Oslo: Universitetsforlaget.

Bauman, Z. (1991) *Modernity and Ambivalence*, Cambridge: Polity Press.

—— (1992) 'Soil, Blood and Identity', *Sociological Review*, 40, 4: 675–701.

BBC2 Northern Ireland (19 September 2009) *Hearts and Minds*.

Beiber, F. (2006) 'After Dayton, Dayton? The Evolution of an Unpopular Peace', *Ethnopolitics*, 5, 1, 15–31.

Bell, C. (2000) *Peace Agreements and Human Rights*, Oxford: Oxford University Press.

—— (2003) 'Dealing with the Past in Northern Ireland', *Fordham International Law Journal*, 26, 1095–1145.

—— (2008) *On the Law of Peace: peace agreements and the lex pacificatoria*, Oxford: Oxford University Press.

Bell, D. (1990) *Acts of Union: youth culture and sectarianism in Northern Ireland*, Basingstoke: Macmillan.

—— (1996) 'Interview', in M. Hyndman (ed.) *Further Afield: journeys from a protestant past*, Belfast: Beyond the Pale Publications.

Benedict, R. (1946) *The Chrysanthemum and the Sword: patterns of Japanese culture*, Boston: Houghton Mifflin.

Benhabib, S. (2002) *The Claims of Culture: equality and diversity in the global era*, Princeton: Princeton University Press.

Bennett, R. (1998) 'Don't Mention the War: culture in Northern Ireland', in D. Miller (ed.) *Rethinking Northern Ireland*, London: Longman.

Bew, P., Gibbon, P. and Patterson, H. (1979) *The State in Northern Ireland 1921–1972*, Manchester: Manchester University Press.

Biden, J. and Gelb, L. (1 May 2006) 'Unity through autonomy in Iraq', *New York Times*.

Bill of Rights Forum (2008) *Final Report, Recommendations to the Northern Ireland Human Rights Commission on a Bill of Rights for Northern Ireland*,

Belfast: NIHRC. Available: http://www.billofrightsforum.org/borf_final_report. pdf (accessed 27 October 2009).

Bose, S. (2002) *Bosnia after Dayton: nationalist partition and international intervention*, London: Hurst.

Bougarel, X., Helms, E. and Duijzings, G. (eds) (2007) *The New Bosnian Mosaic: identities, memories and moral claims in a post-war society*, Aldershot: Ashgate.

Brenner, N. (1994) 'Foucault's New Functionalism', *Theory and Society*, 23: 679–709.

Brown, T. (1985) *The Whole Protestant Community: the making of a historical myth*, Derry: Field Day.

—— (1992) 'Identities in Ireland: the historical perspective', in J. Lundy and A. Mac Póilin (eds) *Styles of Belonging: the cultural identities of Ulster*, Belfast: Lagan Press.

Brown, W. (1995) *States of Injury: power and freedom in late modernity*, Princeton New Jersey: Princeton University Press.

Brubaker, R. (2002) 'Ethnicity Without Groups', *Archives Européennes de Sociologie*, XLII, 2, 163–89.

—— (2004) *Ethnicity Without Groups*, Harvard: Harvard University Press.

Brubaker, R. and Cooper, F. (2000) 'Beyond "Identity"', *Theory & Society*, 29, 1–47.

Bryan, D. (2006) 'The Politics of Community', *Critical Review of International Social and Political Philosophy*, 9, 4, 603–17.

Bryan, D. and Stevenson, C. (2009) *Flags Monitoring Project 2008*, Institute of Irish Studies, The Queen's University of Belfast, Good Relations and Reconciliation Publications, Office of the First Minister and Deputy First Minister. Available: http://www.ofmdfmni.gov.uk/gr-pub (accessed 6 December 2009).

Buckley, A. D. (2008) 'Ethnology in the North of Ireland', in M. Nic Craith, R. Johler and U. Kockel (eds) *Everyday Culture in Europe: approaches and methodologies*, Aldershot: Ashgate.

Burton, F. (1978) *The Politics of Legitimacy: struggles in a Belfast community*, London: Routledge and Kegan Paul.

Butler, J. (1993) *Bodies That Matter*, London and New York: Routledge.

—— (2004) *Undoing Gender*, London and New York: Routledge.

—— (2006) *Precarious Life: the powers of mourning and violence*, London: Verso.

Butler, J. and Scott J. W. (eds) (1992) *Feminists Theorize the Political*, London and New York: Routledge.

Calhoun, C. (1997) *Nationalism*, Buckingham: Open University Press.

Campbell, D. (1999) 'Apartheid Cartography: the political anthropology and spatial effects of international diplomacy in Bosnia', *Political Geography*, 18, 395–435.

Campbell, S. (2007) '"Pack Up Your Troubles": politics & popular music in pre- & post-ceasefire Ulster', *Popular Musicology Online*, 4. Available: http://www.popular-musicology-online.com/issues/04/campbell-01.html (accessed 11 December 2009).

Čekrlija, D. (2007) 'On the Primacy of Ethnic Identity', *Proceedings from the*

Conference Examples of Bosnia and Herzegovina: sustainable concepts or lost ways of the international community, Sarajevo: Heinrich Boll Foundation and Office for Bosnia and Herzegovina.

Chandler, D. (2000) *Bosnia: faking democracy after Dayton*, London: Pluto Press.

Chen-Xiaomei (1996) *Occidentalism: a theory of counter discourse in post-Maoist China*, Oxford: Oxford University Press.

Church, C., Visser, A. and Shepherd-Johnson, L. (2004) 'A Path to Peace or Persistence? The "Single Identity" Approach to Conflict Resolution in Northern Ireland', *Conflict Resolution Quarterly*, 21, 3: 269–93.

Clancy, P., Drudy, S., Lynch, K. and O'Dowd, L. (eds) (1986) *Ireland: a sociological profile*, Dublin: Institute for Public Administration.

Cohen, A. P. (1985) *The Symbolic Construction of Community*, London: Tavistock and Harwood.

Committee of the Presbyterian Church in Ireland on National and International Problems (c. 1980) *Republicanism, Loyalism and Pluralism in Ireland*, Belfast: General Assembly of the Presbyterian Church in Ireland.

Coogan, T. P. (19 September 1999) *Ireland on Sunday*.

Cook-Huffman, C. (2009) 'The Role of Identity in Conflict', in D. J. D. Sandole, S. Byrne, I. Sandole-Staroste and J. Senehi (eds) *Handbook of Conflict Analysis and Resolution*, London and New York: Routledge.

Council of Europe (1995) Framework Convention for the Protection of National Minorities, Strasbourg. Available: http://conventions.coe.int/Treaty/EN/Treaties/Html/157.htm (accessed 15 October 2009).

Cowan, J. K. (2006) 'Culture and Rights after *Culture and Rights*', *American Anthropologist*, 108, 1, 9–24.

Cowan, J. K., Dembour, M.-B. and Wilson, R. A. (eds) (2001) *Culture and Rights Anthropological Perspectives*, Cambridge: Cambridge University Press.

Darby, J. and MacGinty (eds) (2003) *Contemporary Peacemaking: conflict, violence and peace processes*, Basingstoke: Palgrave MacMillan.

Dayton Peace Accords (1995) Available: http://www.state.gov/www/regions/eur/bosnia/bosagree.html (accessed 7 October 2009).

Dean, M. (1994) *Critical and Effective Histories: Foucault's methods and historical sociology*, London and New York: Routledge.

Deane, S. (1984) *Heroic Styles: the tradition of an idea*, Pamphlet No 4, Derry: Field Day.

—— (1997) *Strange Country: modernity and nationhood in Irish writing since 1790*, Oxford: Clarendon.

Delanty, G. (2004) 'From Nationality to Citizenship: cultural identity and cosmopolitan challenges in Ireland', in A. Finlay (ed.) (2004) *Nationalism and Multiculturalism: Irish identity, citizenship and the peace process*, Münster: LIT Verlag.

Delanty, G. and O'Mahony, P. (2002) *Nationalism and Social Theory*, London: Sage.

Department of Education Northern Ireland (2009) *Programmes of Study and Attainment Targets, Educational (Cross-Curricular) Themes*. Available: http://ww.denic.gov.uk/cct_1.pdf (accessed 16 January 2009).

Devine F. (1989) 'Letting Labour Lead: Jack Macgougan and the pursuit of unity, 1913–58', *Saothar, Journal of the Irish Labour History Society*, 14, 113–24.

—— (1997) 'Navigating a Lone Channel: Stephen McGonagle, trade unionism and labour politics in Derry 1914–97', *Saothar, Journal of the Irish Labour History Society*, 22: 139–52.

Dickson, B. (2009) 'Where Now for the Bill of Rights?' *Fortnight*, 11 (March 2009).

Dizdarevic, S. (2004) *The Constitution of Bosnia and Herzegovina – Towards New Solutions*, Open Society Fund Bosnia and Herzegovina. Available: http://www.soros.org.ba/!en/pravo_ustav_bih_01.htm 4/7/07 (accessed 17 September 2008).

Donnan, H. and McFarlane, G. (1983) 'Informal Social Organisation', in J. Darby (ed.) *Northern Ireland – the background to the conflict*, Belfast: Appletree Press.

—— (ed.) (1997) *Culture and Policy in Northern Ireland – anthropology in the public arena*, Belfast: Institute of Irish Studies.

Dreyfus, H. L. and Rabinow, P. (1982) *Michel Foucault: beyond structuralism and hermeneutics*, Harvester Wheatsheaf.

Duffy, M. and Evans, G. (1996) 'Building Bridges? The Political Implications of Electoral Integration for Northern Ireland', *British Journal of Political Science*, 26, 123–42.

Dzenovska, D. (2006) 'Negotiating the Threshold of Difference: multiculturalism and other national things in Latvia', a paper presented at *European Association of Social Anthropologists 9th biennial conference: Europe and the world*, University of Bristol 18–21 September 2006.

Edkins, J. (2006) 'The Local, the Global and the Troubling', *Critical Review of International Social and Political Philosophy*, 9, 4: 499–511.

Edwards, A. (2007a) 'Interpreting the Conflict in Northern Ireland', *Ethnopolitics*, 6, 1: 137–44.

—— (2007b) 'Democratic Socialism and Sectarianism: the Northern Ireland Labour Party and Progressive Unionist Party', *Politics*, 27, 1, 24–31.

—— (2009) *A History of the Northern Ireland Labour Party: democratic socialism and sectarianism*, Manchester: Manchester University Press.

Edwards, A. and Bloomer, S. (eds) (2008) *Transforming the Peace Process in Northern Ireland: from terrorism to democratic politics?* Dublin: Irish Academic Press.

Eriksen, T. H. (2001) 'Between Universalism and Relativism: a critique of the UNESCO concept of culture', in J. K. Cowan, M.-B. Dembour and R. A. Wilson (eds) *Culture and Rights: anthropological perspectives*, Cambridge: Cambridge University Press.

Erikson, E. (1968) *Identity: youth and crisis*, New York: Norton.

Esman, M. J. (2004) *An Introduction to Ethnic Conflict*, Cambridge: Polity Press.

Executive Board of the American Anthropological Association, 'Statement on Human Rights Submitted to the United Nations Commission on Human Rights (1947)', *American Anthropologist*, 49, 4: 539–43.

Farrell, M. (1980) *Northern Ireland: the orange state*, 2nd edn, London: Pluto Press.

Farry, S. (2009) 'Consociationalism and the Creation of a Shared Future for Northern Ireland', in R. Taylor (ed.) *Consociational Theory: McGarry and O'Leary and the Northern Ireland conflict*, London and New York: Routledge.

Fearon, K. (1999) *Women's Work: the story of the Northern Ireland Women's Coalition*, Belfast: Blackstaff Press.

Fearon, K. and McWilliams, M. (2000) 'Swimming Against the Mainstream: the Northern Ireland Women's Coalition', in R. Roulston and C. Davies (eds) *Gender, Democracy and Inclusion in Northern Ireland*, Basingstoke: Palgrave.

Feeney, B. (2009) Review of Edwards A. (2009) 'A History of the Northern Ireland Labour Party: democratic socialism and sectarianism', Manchester: Manchester University Press, *History Ireland*, 17, 4, 59.

Feldman, A. (1991) *Formations of Violence: the narrative of the body and political terror in Northern Ireland*, Chicago and London: University of Chicago Press.

Finlay, A. (1989) 'Trade Unionism and Sectarianism Among Derry Shirt Workers 1920–68', unpublished PhD Thesis, University of London.

—— (1992) 'Work To Be Done: workplace sectarianism defies simple answers', *Fortnight*, 305, 6–7.

—— (1993) 'Sectarianism in the Workplace: the case of the Derry shirt industry 1868–1968', *Irish Journal of Sociology*, 3, 79–93.

—— (1998) *ATGWU Action Programme – working for equality final report*, Unpublished Evaluation Report, Amalgamated Transport and General Workers Union and the Central Community Relations Unit.

—— (1999) '"Whatever You Say Say Nothing" – an ethnographic encounter in Northern Ireland and its sequel', *Sociological Research Online*, 4, 3. Available: http://www.socresonline.org.uk/socresonline/4/3/finlay.html (accessed 3 December 2009).

—— (2001a) 'Defeatism and Northern Protestant "Identity"', *The Global Review of Ethnopolitics*, 1, 2, 3–20. Available: http://www.ethnopolitics.org (accessed 9 September 2008).

—— (2001b) 'Reflexivity, the Dilemmas of Identification and an Ethnographic Encounter in Northern Ireland', in M. Smyth and G. Robinson (eds) *Researching Violent Societies: ethical and methodological issues*, Tokyo and London: United Nations University Press and Pluto Press.

—— (ed.) (2004) *Nationalism and Multiculturalism: Irish identity, citizenship and the peace process*, Münster: LIT Verlag.

—— (2006) 'Anthropology Misapplied? The Culture Concept and the Peace Process in Ireland', *Anthropology in Action*, 13, 1–2, 1–10.

—— (2007) 'Irish Studies, Cultural Pluralism and the Peace Process', *Irish Studies Review*, 15, 2.

—— (2008) 'The Persistence of the Old Idea of Culture, the Peace Process in Ireland and Anthropology', *Critique of Anthropology*, 28, 3, 279–96.

Finlay, P. (4 June 2004) 'Equality Should be Cornerstone of Law on Citizenship', *The Irish Times*. Available: http://www.ireland.com/newspaper/opinion/2004/0604/41347564380 (accessed 1 August 2004).

FitzGerald, G. (1976) 'Ireland's Identity Problems', *Études Irelandaises*, 1 (December): 135–42.

—— (1991) *All in a Life*, London: Papermak.

—— (1997) 'Vision of Northern Ireland Catholics Outbreeding Protestants is a Dangerous Myth', *The Irish Times*, 26 July 1997.

Foster, R. (1989) 'Varieties of Irishness', in M. Crozier (ed.) *Cultural Traditions in Northern Ireland*, Belfast: Institute of Irish Studies.

Foucault, M. (1980) *The History of Sexuality Volume I: an introduction*, New York: Vintage Books.

—— (1982) 'Afterword: the subject and power', in H. L. Dreyfus and P. Rabinow (eds) *Michel Foucault: beyond structuralism and hermeneutics*, Brighton: Harvester Wheatsheaf.

—— (1991) *Discipline and Punish: the birth of the prison*, London: Allen Lane.

—— (2003) *Society Must Be Defended: lectures at the Collège de France 1975– 1976*, trans. D. Macey (ed.), Arnold Davidson. New York: Picador.

—— (2007) *Security, Territory, Population: lectures at the Collège de France 1977–1978*, M. Senellart (ed.) Basingstoke: Palgrave Macmillan.

Frazer, H. and Fitzduff, M. (1994) *Improving Community Relations*, Belfast: Community Relations Council.

Friel, L. (16 January 2002) 'Now You See It, Now You Don't: the unionist majority, the census and the electoral register', *An Phoblacht Republican News*.

Gallagher, M. (1995) 'How Many Nations Are There in Ireland?', *Ethnic and Racial Studies*, 18, 4: 715–39.

Gandhi, L. (2006) *Affective Communities: anticolonial thought, fin-de-siècle radicalism, and the politics of friendship*, Durham and London: Duke University Press.

Geertz, C. (1964) 'A Study of National Character (Book Review)', *Economic Development and Cultural Change*, 12, 2, 205–09.

Gibbons, L. (1996) *Transformations in Irish Culture*, Cork: Cork University Press.

Gilmore, A. (May 2008) 'What Next For the Bill of Rights', *Fortnight*, 459: 15.

Gilroy, P. (1990) 'Nationalism, History and Ethnic Absolutism', *History Workshop Journal*, 30, 1: 114–20.

—— (2004) *After Empire: melancholia or convivial culture?* London and New York: Routledge.

Gleason, Phillip (1983) 'Identifying Identity: a semantic history', *The Journal of American History*, 69, 4, 910–31.

Gonzalez, R. J. (2007) 'Towards Mercenary Anthropology? The New US Army Counterinsurgency Manual FM 3–24 and the Military-Anthropology Complex', *Anthropology Today*, 23, 3.

—— (2008) 'Human Terrain: past, present and future applications', *Anthropology Today*, 24, 1.

—— (2009) 'Going "Tribal": Notes on pacification in the 21st century', *Anthropology Today*, 25, 2.

The Government of the United Kingdom of Great Britain and Northern Ireland and the

Government of Ireland (1998) *Agreement Reached in the Multi-Party Negotiations*, Belfast: Her Majesty's Stationary Office.

Graham, B. and Nash, C. (2006) 'A Shared Future: territoriality, pluralism and public policy in Northern Ireland', *Political Geography*, 25, 253–78.

Gray, M. (1986) 'Reminiscence: a shop steward remembers', *Saothar, Journal of the Irish Labour History Society*, 11: 109–15.

Gregory, D. (2008) '"The Rush to the Intimate": counterinsurgency and the cultural turn', *Radical Philosophy*, 150, 8–23.

Gudgin, G. (2002) 'Reports of the End of Protestant Domination Exaggerated', *The Irish Times*, 15 February 2002.

Gutmann, A. (ed.) (1994) *Multiculturalism: examining the politics of recognition*, Princeton N.J.: Princeton University Press.

Hadden, T. (2008) 'Look to the Future', *Fortnight*, 461: 9.

Hall, S. (1996) 'Who Needs Identity?' in S. Hall, and P. du Gay (eds) *Questions of Cultural Identity*, London: Sage.

—— (2000) 'Conclusion: the multicultural question', in B. Hesse (ed.) *Un/Settled Muliculturalisms: diasporas, entanglements, 'transruptions'*, London: Zed Books.

Hanf, T. (1981) 'The Political Secularization Issue in Lebanon', *Annual Review of the Social Science of Religion*, 5, 249.

Hardt, M. and Negri, A. (2000) *Empire*, Cambridge, Massachusetts: Harvard University Press.

Harris, R. (1986, 1972) *Prejudice and Tolerance in Ulster: a study of neighbours and 'strangers' in a border community*, Manchester: Manchester University Press.

Harvey, C. (2003) 'Sticking to the Terms of the Agreement', *Fortnight*, 416: 9.

Hastrup, K. (ed.) (2001) *Legal Cultures and Human Rights*, London: De Hague.

Helsinki Committee for Human Rights in Bosnia and Herzegovina (2005a) *Strategy for Operation of the Helsinki Committee for Human Rights in Bosnia and Herzegovena for the period 2005–2010*, Helsinki Committee for Human Rights in Bosnia and Herzegovina: Sarajevo. Available: http://www.bh-chr.org/Reports/ Strategy%20for%20Operation %20of%20the%20HCHR%20in%20BH%20for% 202005–10.htm (accessed 4 September 2007).

—— (2005b) *Report of an International Conference Achievements in the Field of Human Rights Ten Years After Dayton*, Sarajevo 10–11 May 2005. Available: http://www.bh-hchr.org/Statements/e10-05-05 (accessed 12 March 2007).

Hennessey, T. and Wilson, R. (1997) *With All Due Respect: pluralism and parity of esteem*, Belfast: Democratic Dialogue Report No 7.

Hodžić, E. (5 July 2006) 'On Human Rights: between cacophony and silence', *Puls demokratije*. Available: http://www.pulsdemokratije.net/clanak.php?sifra = 060705004&lang = en (accessed 12 June 2007).

—— (27 September 2006) 'Truth and Reconciliation Commission II: a forum to end myth-making', *Puls demokratije*. Available: http://www.pulsdemokratije.net/ index.php?&l = en&id = 380 (accessed 23 November 2009).

Honneth, A. (1995) *The Struggle for Recognition*, Cambridge: Polity.

Horowitz, D. (2001). 'The Northern Ireland Agreement: clear, consociational, and risky', in J. McGarry (ed.) *Northern Ireland and the Divided World: post-agreement Northern Ireland in comparative perspective*, Oxford: Oxford University Press.

Hyndman, M. (1996) *Further Afield: journeys from a Protestant past*, Belfast: Beyond the Pale Publications.

Ibrahimagic, O. (2001) *Srpsko osporavanje Bosne i Bosnjaka*, Sarajevo: VKBI.

Ignatieff, M. (1993) *Blood and Belonging: journeys into the new nationalism*, London: Vintage.

Inda, J. X. (2005) 'Analytics of the Modern: an introduction', in J. X. Inda (ed.) *Anthropologies of Modernity: Foucault, governmentality, and life politics*, Oxford: Blackwell.

International Crisis Group (12 November 2009) *Bosnia's Dual Crisis Policy Briefing Europe Briefing*, 57. International Crisis Group: Sarajevo/Brussels.

Jansen, S. (2000) 'Anti-Nationalism: post-Yugoslav resistance and narratives of self and society'. Unpublished PhD thesis, University of Hull.

—— (2001) 'The Streets of Beograd: urban space and protest identities in Serbia', *Political Geography*, 20, 35–55.

Jardine, E. F. (1994) 'Demographic Structure in Northern Ireland and its Implications for Constitutional Preference', *Journal of the Statistical and Social Inquiry Society of Ireland*, XXVII, 1, 193–220.

Jarman, N. (1996) *Material Conflicts: parades and visual displays in Northern Ireland*, Oxford: Berg.

—— (2006) 'Policing Policy and Practices: responding to disorder in north Belfast', *Anthropology in Action*, 13, 1&2: 11–21.

Jenkins, R. (1996) *Social Identity*, London and New York: Routledge.

—— (1997) *Rethinking Ethnicity: arguments and explorations*, London: Sage.

—— (2005) 'Groups and Group Rights: real or imaginary', *10th Torkel Opsahl Memorial Lecture*, Belfast: Democratic Dialogue, 1–17 (1 December 2005).

—— (2006) 'When Politics and Social Theory Converge: group identification and group rights in Northern Ireland', *Nationalism and Ethnic Politics*, 12: 389–410.

Joppke, C. (2004) 'The Retreat of Multiculturalism in the Liberal State: theory and policy', *The British Journal of Sociology*, 55, 1: 237–57.

Kalender, A. (5 February 2008) 'A Different Dialogue Between Culture and Policy: challenges for the development of cultural policy in Bosnia-Herzegovenia', *Puls demokratije*. Available: http://www.pulsdemokratije.net/index.php?id = 712&l = en (accessed 12 November 2008).

Kerr, M. (2005) *Imposing Power Sharing: conflict and coexistence in Northern Ireland and Lebanon*, Dublin: Irish Academic Press.

Kiberd, D. (2000) *Irish Classics*, London: Penguin.

Kilcullen, D. (2007) 'Ethics, Politics and Non-State Warfare: a response to Gonzalez', *Anthropology Today*, 23, 3.

Kosovan Nansen Dialogue (2007) Available: http://www.kndialogue.org/ (accessed 3 December 2009).

Kymlicka, W. (ed.) (1995) *The Rights of Minority Cultures*, Oxford: Oxford University Press.

Lake, D. A. and Rothchild, D. S. (1998) 'Spreading Fear: the genesis of transnational ethnic conflict', in D. A. Lake and D. S. Rothchild (eds) *The International Spread of Ethnic Conflict: fear, diffusion, and escalation*, Princeton, N.J.: Princeton University Press.

Landry, C. (2002) 'Togetherness in Difference: culture at the cross roads in Bosnia-Herzegovina', Strasbourg: Council of Europe.

Langhammer, M. (11 October 2000) 'Assembly Voting System Referred to Human Rights Commission', *Labour Press Release*.

Langlois, T. (2000) 'Culture, Diversity and Access', *Fortnight*, 390: 18–19.

Lijphart, A. (1975) 'The Northern Ireland Problem', *The British Journal of Political Science*, 5, 3: 83–106.

—— (1977) *Democracy in Plural Societies: a comparative exploration*, New Haven and London: Yale University Press.

—— (1995) 'Self-Determination versus Pre-Determination of Ethnic Minorities in Power-Sharing Systems', in W. Kymlicka (ed.) *The Rights of Minority Cultures*, Oxford: Oxford University Press.

Little, A. (20 October 2005) 'Return to Sarajevo – Part 2 Mostar', *BBC World Service*. Available: http://news.bbc.co.uk/2/hi/programmes/documentary_archive/4361420. stm (accessed 20 July 2006).

Loomba, A. (1998) *Colonialism/Postcolonialism*, London and New York: Routledge.

Loyd, A. (1999) *My War Gone By, I Miss It So*, New York: Penguin Books.

Lutz, C. (2008) 'Selling Ourselves the Perils of Pentagon Funding for Anthropology', *Anthropology Today*, 24, 5, 1–3.

Lyons, F. S. L. (1979) *Culture and Anarchy in Ireland 1890–1939*, Oxford: Oxford University Press.

Marcon, G., Andreis, S., Bonacker, T., Braun, C., Nicora, F., Pellizzer, V. and Skjelsbaer, I. (2008) 'Conflict Society and the Transformation of the Bosnia-Herzegovina Question, Case Study Report', *Working Paper 5 SHUR: Human Rights in Conflicts: the role of civil society*, Oslo International Peace Research Institute – PRIO, the Marburg University's Centre of Conflict Studies and Lunaria.

Margalit, A. and Raz, J. (1995) 'National Self-Determination', in J. W. Kymlicka (ed.) *The Rights of Minority Cultures*, Oxford: Oxford University Press.

Markell, P. (2003) *Bound by Recognition*, New Jersey: Princeton University Press.

Marx, K. (1859; 1987) *The Eighteenth Brumaire of Louis Napoleon*, London: Lawrence Wishart.

McAleese, M. (2001) 'Foreword', in A. Pollak (ed.) *Multi-Culturalism: The view from the two Irelands*, Cork: Cork University Press and the Centre for Cross-Border Studies.

McCabe, B. (2006) 'Ten Years of Women's Politics', *Fortnight*, 445, 7.

McCann, E. (28 February 2001) 'To See Ourselves As "Others" See Us', *Belfast Telegraph*.

McCrudden, C. (2006) 'Consociationalism, Equality and Minorities in the Northern Ireland Bill of Rights Debate', *Legal Studies Research Paper, Working Paper 6*, University of Oxford Faculty of Law.

—— (2007) 'Consociationalism, Equality, and Minorities in the Northern Ireland Bill of Rights Debate: the role of the OSCE High Commissioner on National Minorities', in J. Morison, K. McEvoy and G. Anthony (eds) *Judges, Transition, and Human Rights*, Oxford: Oxford University Press.

—— (2008) 'First Do No Harm', *Fortnight*, 461: 8.

McDonald, H. (2004) 'Remembering Mairtin', *Fortnight*, 422, 28–29.

McFate, M. (2007) 'Building Bridges or Burning Heretics? A Response to Gonzalez', *Anthropology Today*, 23, 3.

McGarry, J. (1998) 'Political Settlements in Northern Ireland and South Africa', *Political Studies*, 46, 5.

McGarry, J. (ed.) (2001) *Northern Ireland and the Divided World: post-agreement Northern Ireland in comparative perspective*, Oxford: Oxford University Press.

McGarry, J. and O'Leary, B. (1995) *Explaining Northern Ireland: broken images*, Oxford: Blackwell.

—— (eds) (2004) *The Northern Ireland Conflict: consociational engagements*, Oxford: Oxford University Press.

—— (2007) 'Iraq's Constitution of 2005: liberal consociation as political prescription', *International Journal of Constitutional Law*, 5, 4: 670–98.

—— (2009) 'Argument', in R. Taylor (ed.) *Consociational Theory: McGarry and O'Leary and the Northern Ireland conflict*, London and New York: Routledge.

Macgougan, J. (1948) *The Londonderry Air*, Belfast, Socialist Forum (Pamphlet reprinted from *Town and Country Planning*), Autumn 1948.

McGrew, A. (2002) 'Liberal Internationalism: between realism and cosmopolitanism', in D. Held and A. McGrew (eds) *Governing Globalization: power, authority and global governance*, Cambridge: Polity Press.

McIntyre, A. (2008) *Good Friday: the death of Irish republicanism*, New York: Ausubo Press.

McKay, S. (2000) *Northern Protestants: an unsettled people*, Belfast: Blackstaff.

McLoone, M. (2004) 'Punk Music in Northern Ireland: the political power of "what might have been"', *Irish Studies Review*, 12, 1, 29–38.

McMahon, P. and Western, J. (2009) 'The Death of Dayton: how to stop Bosnia from falling apart', *Foreign Affairs*, 88, 5: 69–83.

McNay, L. (1992) *Foucault and Feminism: power, gender and the self*, Boston: Northeastern University Press.

McVeigh, R. (2002) 'Between Reconciliation and Pacification: the British State and community relations in the north of Ireland', *Community Development Journal*, 37, 1: 47–59.

McVeigh, R. and Rolston, B. (2007) 'From Good Friday to Good Relations: sectarianism, racism and the Northern Ireland state', *Race and Class*, 48, 4: 1–23.

McWilliams, M. and Finlay, A. (1992) *ATGWU Action Programme – Working for Equality: interim evaluation report*, University of Ulster.

Memmi, A. (1990) *The Colonizer and the Colonized*, London: Earth Scan.

Merry, S. E. (2003) 'Human Rights Law and the Demonization of Culture (and Anthropology Along the Way)', *Polar: Political and Legal Anthropology Review*, 26, 1: 156–74.

Milotte, M. (1984) *Communism in Modern Ireland: the pursuit of a workers republic*, Humanities Press.

Minority Rights Group (20 November 2006) 'Many Electoral Systems Across the World Still Exclude Minorities – new MRG report', Minority Rights Group Press Release. Available: http://www.minorityrights.org/?lid = 674 (accessed 4 September 2007).

——(18 February 2007) 'Jew Contests Prohibition on Minorities Contesting Bosnian Presidency', Minority Rights Group Press Release. Available: http//www.minorityrights.org/?lid = 1796 (accessed 4 November 2007).

Minority Rights Group and Association of Citizens for Human Rights Protection 'ZGP' Mostar (2001) *Workshop on the Decision of the Constitutional Court of Bosnia and Herzegovina on the Constituent Status of Peoples and the Process of Return*, Mostar 16–17 November 2001. Available: http://www.minorityrights.org/ WorkshopReports/work_repchapterdetailprinter. asp?ID = 96 (accessed 12 March 2007).

Morel, C. (1 July 2006) *Notes from Sarajevo*, Minority Rights Group. Available: http://www.minorityrights.org/?lid = 690 (accessed 4 September 2007).

Morrissey, H. (1983) 'Betty Sinclair: a woman's fight for socialism, 1910–81', *Saothar, Journal of the Irish Labour History Society*, 9: 121–32.

Mujkic, A. (2007) 'We, the Citizens of Ethnopolis', *Constellations*,14, 1: 112–28.

—— (19 November 2007) 'The Spectre of Liberal Democracy is Haunting Bosnia', *Puls demokratije*. Available: http://www.pulsdemokratije.net/index.php?id = 571&1 = en (accessed 17 November 2009).

Muldoon, P. (2003) 'Alternative Ulster: Stiff Little Fingers', in S. Hackett and R. West (eds) *Belfast Songs*, Belfast: Factotum.

Munoz, J. E. (1999) *Disidentifications: queers of color and the performance of politics*, Minneapolis: University of Minnesota Press.

Murphy, D. (2008) 'The Gift and Collective Effervescence: bloodletting and drinking at a black metal festival', Anthropological Research Imperatives, Anthropological Association of Ireland, National University of Ireland, Maynooth, 11 April 2008.

Murtagh, C. (2008) 'A Transient Transition: the cultural and institutional obstacles impeding the Northern Ireland Women's Coalition in its progression from informal to formal politics', *Irish Political Studies*, 23, 1: 21–40.

Nairn, T. (1977) *The Break-up of Britain*, London: Verso.

Nash, C. (2005) 'Equity, Diversity and Interdependence: cultural policy in Northern Ireland', *Antipode*, 37, 272–300.

Nic Craith, M. (2002) *Plural Identities, Singular Narratives: the case of Northern Ireland*, New York: Berghan Books.

Northern Ireland Human Rights Commission (2008) *A Bill of Rights for Northern*

Ireland Advice to the Secretary of State for Northern Ireland, Belfast: Northern Ireland Human Rights Commission, 10 December 2008.

Northern Ireland Women's Coalition (2003) *Change the Face of Politics: Women's Coalition Manifesto 2003*, Belfast: Northern Ireland Women's Coalition.

Office of the First Minister and Deputy First Minister (2004) *Good Relations Policy And Strategic Framework For Northern Ireland*, Belfast: Office of the First Minister and Deputy First Minister. Available: www.sharedfutureni.gov.uk (accessed 8 November 2009).

—— (2005a) *A Shared Future: policy and strategic framework for good relations in Northern Ireland*, Belfast: Office of the First Minister and Deputy First Minister.

—— (2005b) *A Racial Equality Strategy for Northern Ireland 2005–10*, Belfast: Office of the First Minister and Deputy First Minister.

—— (2007) *Good Relations Indicators Baseline Report*, Belfast: Office of the First Minister and Deputy First Minister. Available: http://www.ofmdfmni.gov.uk/index/equality/ (accessed 8 November 2009).

O'Broin, M. (2008) 'Governing Conflict: government and conflict transformation', paper presented at a *School of Politics, International Studies and Philosophy, Queens University, Conference: transformation and the dynamics of social change*, Belfast 28–29 November, 2008.

O'Doherty, M. (5 November 2001) 'A Chance to Sneer at Sectarianism', *Belfast Telegraph*.

O'Dowd, L. (1990) 'Introduction', in A. Memmi (ed.) *The Colonizer and the Colonized*, London: Earth Scan.

—— (1991) 'Intellectuals and Political Culture: a unionist-nationalist comparison', in E. Hughes (ed.) *Culture and Politics in Northern Ireland, 1960–1990*, Milton Keynes: Open University Press.

O'Dowd, L., Rolston, R. and Tomlinson, M. (1980) *Northern Ireland Between Civil Rights and Civil War*, London: CSE Books.

O'Flynn, I. and Russell, D. (2005) *Power Sharing: new challenges for divided societies*, London: Pluto Press.

O'Halloran, C. (1987) *Partition and the Limits of Irish Nationalism an Ideology Under Stress*, Dublin: Gill and Macmillan.

O'Hanlon, M. E. (27/8/06) 'Voluntary Ethnic Re-location in Iraq', *Los Angeles Times*. Available: http://www.mafhoum.com/press9/285S23.htm (accessed 6 June 2008).

O'Leary, B. (2004) 'The Nature of the Agreement', in J. McGarry and B. O'Leary (eds) *The Northern Ireland Conflict: consociational engagements*, Oxford: Oxford University Press.

—— (2006) 'The Realism of Power-Sharing', Foreword to M. Kerr, *Imposing Power-Sharing: conflict and coexistence in Northern Ireland and Lebanon*, Dublin: Irish Academic Press.

—— (2008) 'A Long March: Paul Bew and Ireland's nations', review of P. Bew, *Ireland: The Politics of Enmity 1789–2006*, Oxford University Press, *Dublin Review of Books*. Available: http://www.drb.ie/apr08_issues/a_long_march.htm (accessed 2 July 2008).

O'Neill, O. (2 June 2009) Review of S. Nelman, *Moral Clarity: a guide for grown up idealists*, Bodley Head, *The Financial Times*.

O'Neill, S. and Trelford, G. (2003) *It Makes You Want to Spit! The Definitive Guide to Punk in Northern Ireland*, Dublin: Reekus Music.

The Open Society Fund – Bosnia and Herzegovina (2007) *The Constitution of Bosnia and Herzegovina – towards new solutions*. Available: http://www.soros.org.ba/!en/pravo_ustav_bih_01.htm 4/7/07 (accessed 6 September 2007).

Orwell, G. (1937) *The Road to Wigan Pier*, London: Victor Gollancz.

Osborne, B. (2002) 'Fascination of Religion Head Count', *British Broadcasting Coporation Northern Ireland News*. Available: http://news.bbc.co.uk/1/hi/northern_ireland/2590023.stm (accessed 9 February 2009).

Ó'Tuathail, G. and Dahlman, C. (2004) 'The Clash of Governmentalities: displacement and return in Bosnia-Herzegovona', in W. Larner and W. Williams (eds) *Global Governmentality: governing international spaces*, London and New York: Routledge.

Patterson, H. (1980) *Class Conflict and Sectarianism: the protestant working class and the Belfast labour movement 1868–1920*, Belfast: Blackstaff Press.

Pécheux, M. (1982) *Language Semantics and Ideology*, New York: St Martin's Press.

Pfaff, W. (2007) 'Manifest Destiny: a new direction for America', *New York Review of Books*, LIV, 2, 54–59 (15 February 2007).

Pickering, P. M. (2006) 'Generating Social Capital for Bridging Ethnic Divisions in the Balkans: case studies of two Bosniak cities', *Ethnic and Racial Studies*, 29, 1: 79–103.

Porobić, N. (2005) (Re) constructing a Deeply Divided Society: peace building lessons from Bosnia and Herzegovina, Unpublished MA Thesis, Department of Political Science, University of Lund.

Porter, P. (2007) 'Good Anthropology, Bad History: the cultural turn in studying war', *Parameters US Army War College Quarterly*, 37, 2, 45–58.

Porter, S. (1996) 'Contra Foucault: soldiers, nurses and power', *Sociology*, 30, 1: 59–78.

Preece, D. M. and Wood, H. R. B. (1968) *Book II of the Modern Geography Series: the British Isles*, 15th edn, London: University Tutorial Press, 1968.

Price, D. H. (2007) 'Anthropology as Lamppost? A Comment on the Counterinsurgency Field Manual', *Anthropology Today*, 23, 6.

—— (2008) *Anthropological Intelligence: the deployment and neglect of American anthropology in the Second World War*, Durham: Duke University Press.

Pugh, M. (2002) 'Maintaining Peace and Security', in D. Held and A. McGrew (eds) *Governing Globalization Power, Authority and Global Governance*, Cambridge: Polity Press.

Rabinow, P. and Rose, N. (12 October 2003) *Thoughts on the Concept of Biopower Today*. Available: http://www.molsci.org/research/publications_pdf/Rose_Rabinow_Biopower_Today.pdf (accessed 27 October 2009).

Ramsay, G. (2008) 'Killaloe: The synchronisation of emotion, the creation of community and the enaction of identity in communal musicking (Why a County Clare burlesque tune has become central to enactions of Ulster loyalist identity)', paper presented at *Annual Conference of the Anthropology Association of Ireland*, National University of Ireland, Maynooth, 11 and 12 April 2008.

Ramsbotham, O., Woodhouse, T. and Miall, H. (2005) *Contemporary Conflict Resolution*, Cambridge: Polity Press.

Robben, C. G. M. (2009) 'Anthropology and the Iraq War: an uncomfortable engagement', *Anthropology Today*, 25, 1.

Rolston, B. (1980) 'Community Politics', in L. O'Dowd, B. Rolston and M. Tomlinson (eds) *Northern Ireland: between civil rights and civil war*, London: CSE Books.

—— (1998) 'What's Wrong with Multiculturalism? Liberalism and the Irish Conflict', in D. Miller (ed.) *Rethinking Northern Ireland*. London: Longman.

—— (2001) '"This is Not a Rebel Song": the Irish conflict and popular music', *Race and Class*, 42, 3: 49–67.

Rooney, K. (1998) 'Institutionalising Division', *Fortnight*, 371: 21.

Rose, N. (1996) 'Genealogy, Identity, History', in S. Hall and P. du Gay (eds) *Questions of Cultural Identity*, London: Sage.

—— (1999) *Powers of Freedom*. Cambridge: Cambridge University Press.

Rowbotham, S. (2009) *Edward Carpenter: a life of liberty and love*, London: Verso.

Russell, D. (2004) 'Who is Fed Up with Either/Ors?', *Fortnight*, 421.

Sahlins, M. (2002) *Waiting for Foucault, Still*, Chicago: Prickly Pear Press.

Sarcevic, E. (1997) *Ustavi i politika*, Sarajevo: VKBI.

Scott, D. (2003) 'Culture in Political Theory', *Political Theory*, 31, 1, 92–115.

Silber, L. and Little, A. (1995) *The Death of Yugoslavia*, London: Penguin and BBC Books.

Simms, B. (n.d.) 'A Squalid Performance', *Irish Pages The Media*, 4, 1, 187–200.

Smith, M. G. (1971) 'Some Developments in the Analytic Framework of Pluralism', in L. Kuper and M. G. Smith (eds) *Pluralism in Africa*, Berkeley: University of California Press.

Smyth, G. (2005) *Noisy Island: a short history of Irish rock*, Cork: Cork University Press.

Standing Advisory Commission on Human Rights (1990) *Religious and Political Discrimination and Equality of Opportunity in Northern Ireland*, London: Her Majesty's Stationary Office.

Stephens, L. and Gourley, S. (14 November 2008) *A History of Northern Ireland Club Culture*. Available: http://www.culturenorthernireland.org/article.aspx?art_id = 334 (accessed 9 July 2009).

Stocking, G. W. (1963) 'Matthew Arnold, E. B. Tylor, and the Uses of Invention', *American Anthropologist*, 65, 783–99.

Swan, S. (2008) 'The Accuracy of the "Ethnic Conflict" Paradigm: a reply to Aaron Edwards', *Politics*, 28, 2, 118–23.

Taylor, C. (1994) 'The Politics of Recognition', in A. Gutman (ed.) *Multiculturalism: examining the politics of recognition*, Princeton: Princeton University Press.

Taylor, R. (2001) 'Northern Ireland: consociation or social transformation?' in J. McGarry (ed.) *Northern Ireland and the Divided World: post-agreement Northern Ireland in comparative perspective*, Oxford: Oxford University Press.

—— (ed.) (2009) *Consociational Theory: McGarry and O'Leary and the Northern Ireland conflict*, London and New York: Routledge.

The Irish Times (25 April 1998) 'Support for deal is growing among IRA rank and file'.

Thomas, N. (1994) *Colonialism's Culture: anthropology, travel and government*, Cambridge: Polity Press.

Todd, J., O'Keefe, T., Rougier, N. and Cañás Bottos, L. (2006) 'Fluid or Frozen: choice and change in ethno-national Identification in Contemporary Northern Ireland', *Nationalism and Ethnic Politics*, 12, 3–4, 323–47.

Tokača, M. (19 November 2006) 'Truth and Reconciliation Commission III: truth as admission and compassion', *Puls demokratije*. Available: http://www.pulsdemokratije.net/index.php?&l = en&id = 382 (accessed 23 November 2009).

Trelford, G. and O'Neil, S. (1998) *It Makes You Want to Spit: punk in Ulster, '77-'82*, Belfast: Punk Appreciation Society.

Tutu, D. M. (1984) *Hope and Suffering: sermons and speeches*, Grand Rapids Michigan: Eerdmans. University of Ulster Press Release, *Segregation May Benefit Psychological Health*. Available: http://news.ulster.ac.uk/releases/2008/3866.html (accessed 1 July 2008).

University of Ulster Press Release (1 July 2008) *Segregation May Benefit Psychological Health*. Available: http//news.ulster.ac.uk/releases/2008/3866.html (accessed 3 March 2010).

Valverde, M. (2007) 'Genealogies of European States: Foucauldian reflections', *Economy and Society*, 36, 1: 159–78.

—— (2008) *Beyond Discipline and Punish: Foucault's challenge to criminology*. Available: http://www.thecarceral.org/valverdeforharcourt08.pdf (accessed 29 October 2009).

Vaughan, M. (1991) *Curing Their Ills: colonial power and African illness*, Cambridge and Stanford: Polity Press and Stanford University Press.

Veyne, P. (2008) *Foucault: sa pensée, sa personne*. Paris, Albin Michel.

Vlaisavljevic, U. (1998) 'Politika znanja i neznanja,' *Odjek*, 2, 22.

Walker, G. (1984) The Life and Times of Jack Beattie, *Obair*, 1984, 14–15.

Whitaker, R. (2004) 'Where Difference Lies: democracy and the ethnographic imagination in Northern Ireland', in A. Finlay (ed.) *Nationalism and Multiculturalism: Irish identity, citizenship and the peace process*, Münster: LIT Verlag.

—— (2010) 'Debating Rights in the New Northern Ireland', *Irish Political Studies*, 25, 1, 23–45.

—— (forthcoming) 'The Politics of Friendship in Feminist Anthropology', *Anthropology in Action*.

Whyte, J. (1990) *Interpreting Northern Ireland*, Oxford: Clarendon.

Wilson, R. (11 January 2001) 'Report of the Bill of Rights Culture and Identity

Working Group', Belfast: NIHRC. Available: http://www.nihrc.org/dms/data/ NIHRC/attachments/dd/files/49/Culture_Identity_Working_Group.doc (accessed 15 May 2009).

—— (2003) 'Am I Me or Am I One of Them? Who Has Rights: groups or people?' *Fortnight*, 414: 11.

—— (2009a) 'Towards Cosmopolitanism? Renewing Irishness in the 21st Century', *Journal of Cross Border Studies*, 4, 91–106.

—— (2009b) 'From Consociationalism to Inter-Culturalism', in R. Taylor (ed.) *Consociational Theory: McGarry and O'Leary and the Northern Ireland conflict*, London and New York: Routledge.

Wilson, R. and Wilford, R. (2003) 'Northern Ireland: a route to stability?' Democratic Dialogue. Available: http://www.devolution.ac.uk/Wilson_&Wilford_paper (accessed 13 May 2003).

Wolf, S. (2006) *Ethnic Conflict*, Oxford: Oxford University Press.

Wren, T. (2002) 'Cultural Identity and Personal Identity', in A. W. Musschnga, W. van Haaften, B. Spieker and M. Slors (eds) *Personal and Moral Identity*, Dordrecht: Kluwer Academic Publishers.

Wright, S, (1998) 'The Politicization of "Culture"', *Anthropology Today*, 14, 1: 7–15.

Žižek, S. (1992) 'East European Liberalism and Its Discontents', *New German Critique*, 57, 25–49.

—— (2000a) 'Da Capo Senza Fine', in J. Butler, E. Laclau and S. Žižek (eds) *Contingency, Hegemony, Universality: contemporary dialogues on the left*, London: Verso.

—— (2000b) *The Ticklish Subject: the absent centre of political ontology*, New York: Verso.

Zulaika J. (2005) 'Epilogue', in B. Aretexaga (ed.) *States of Terror: Begona Aretxaga's essays*, Centre for Basque Studies Occasional Paper Series 10, Reno: University of Nevada.

—— (1999) Enemigos, no hay enemigo (Polémicas, imposturas, confesiones post-ETA), Donostia: Erein.

Index